Pattern Pleasure

Lily Frizz

ISBN-10: 1522950184

ISBN-13: 978-152295189

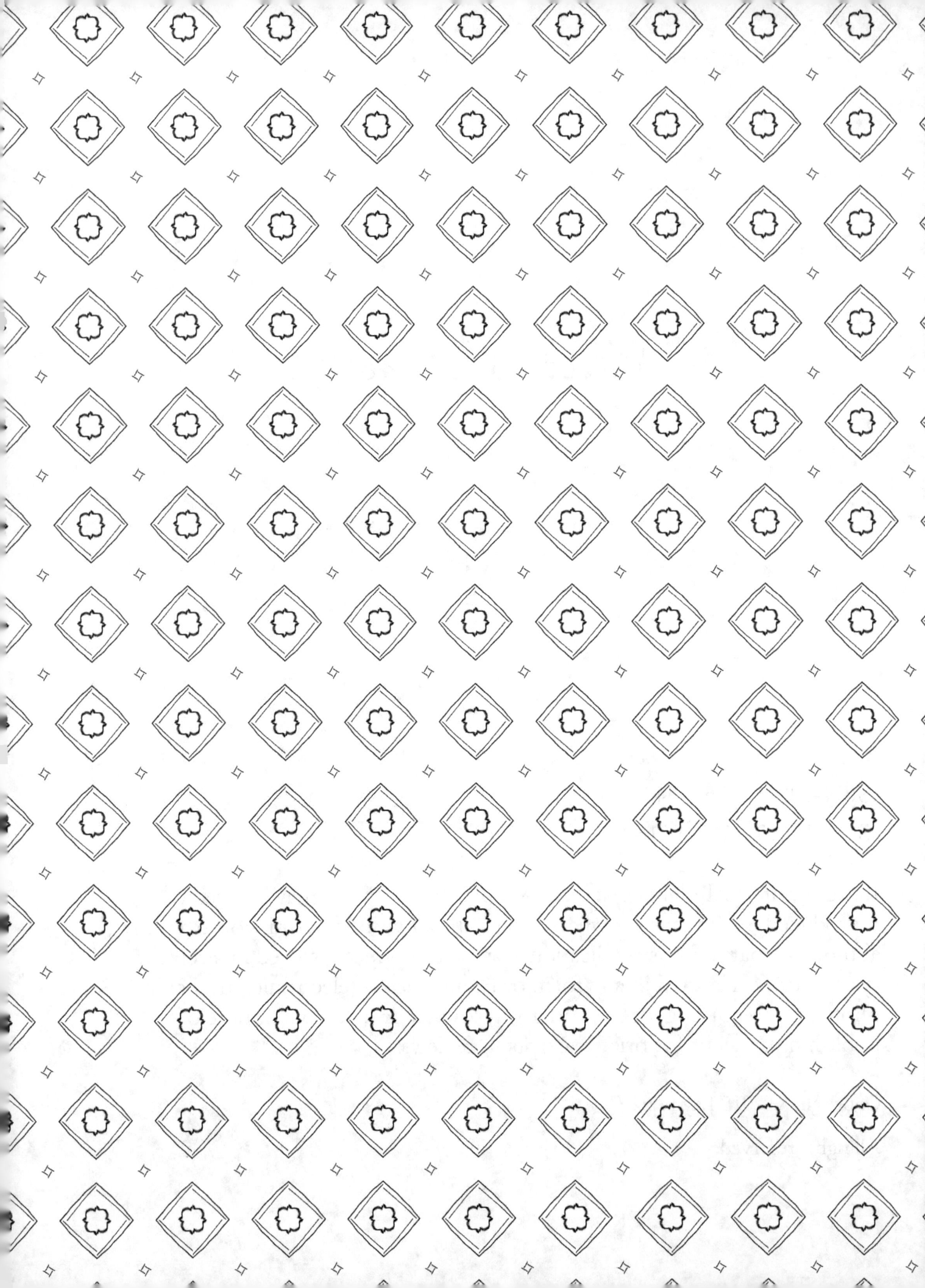

This book belongs to:

_____

Dated:

_____

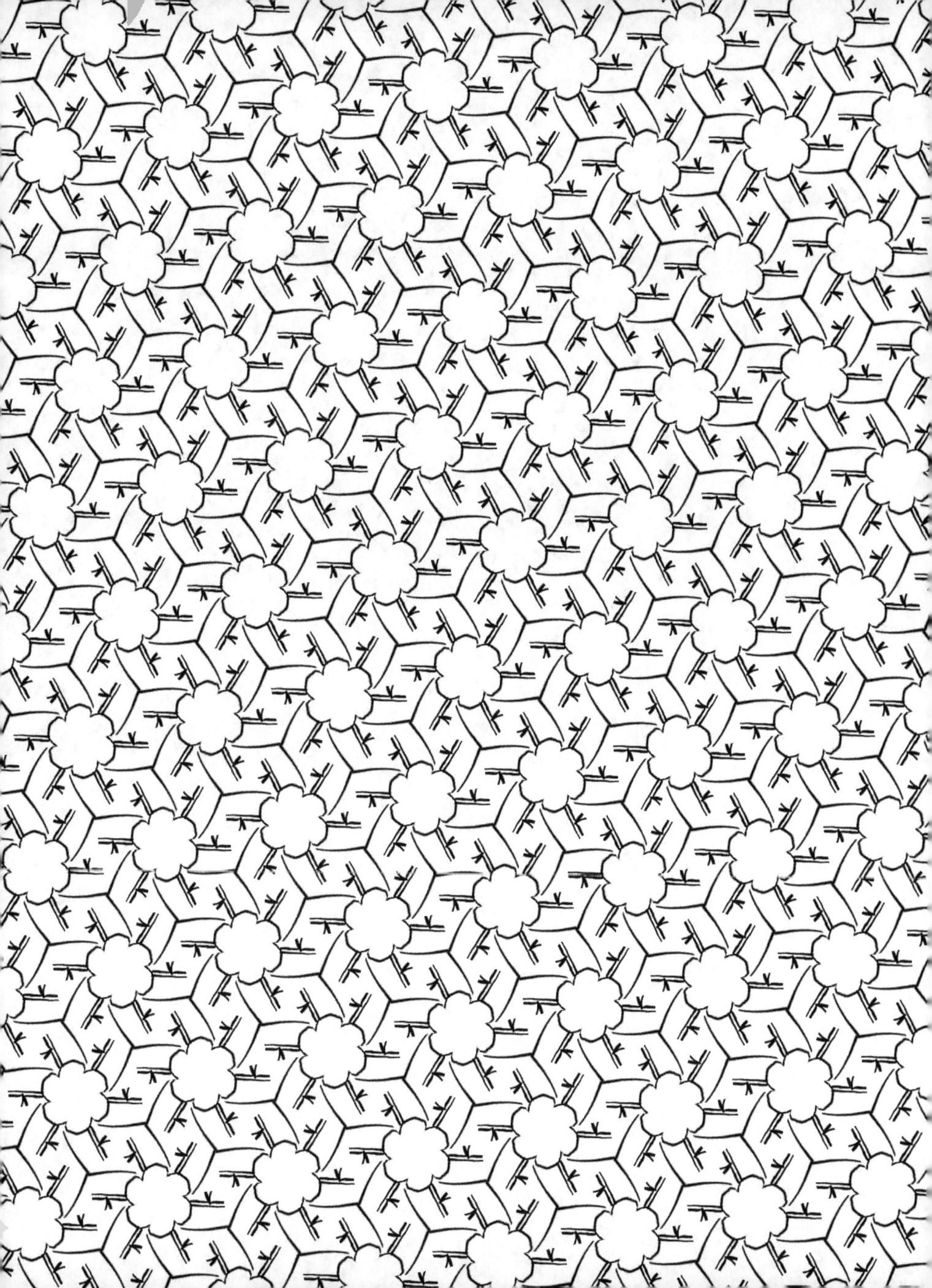

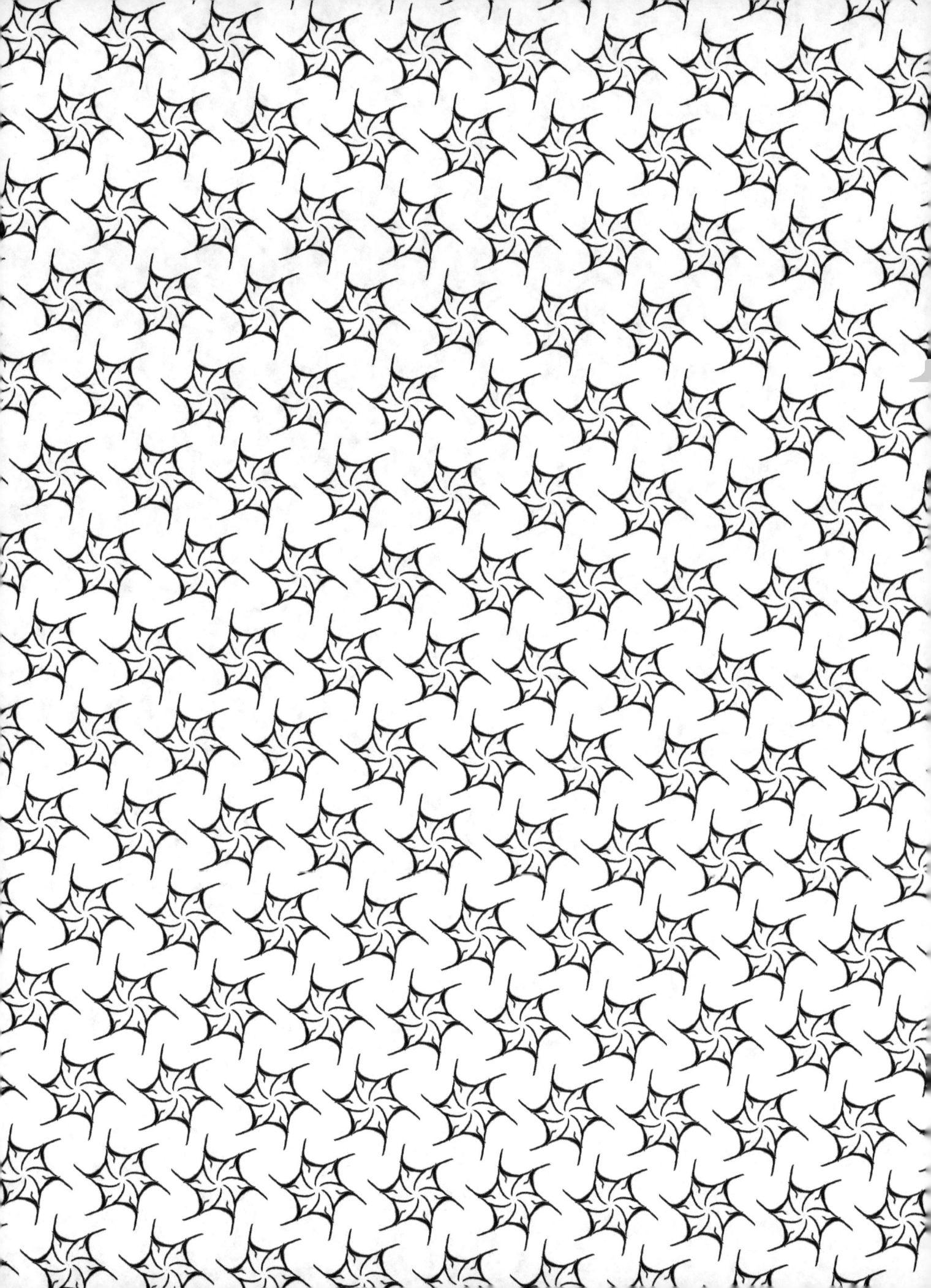

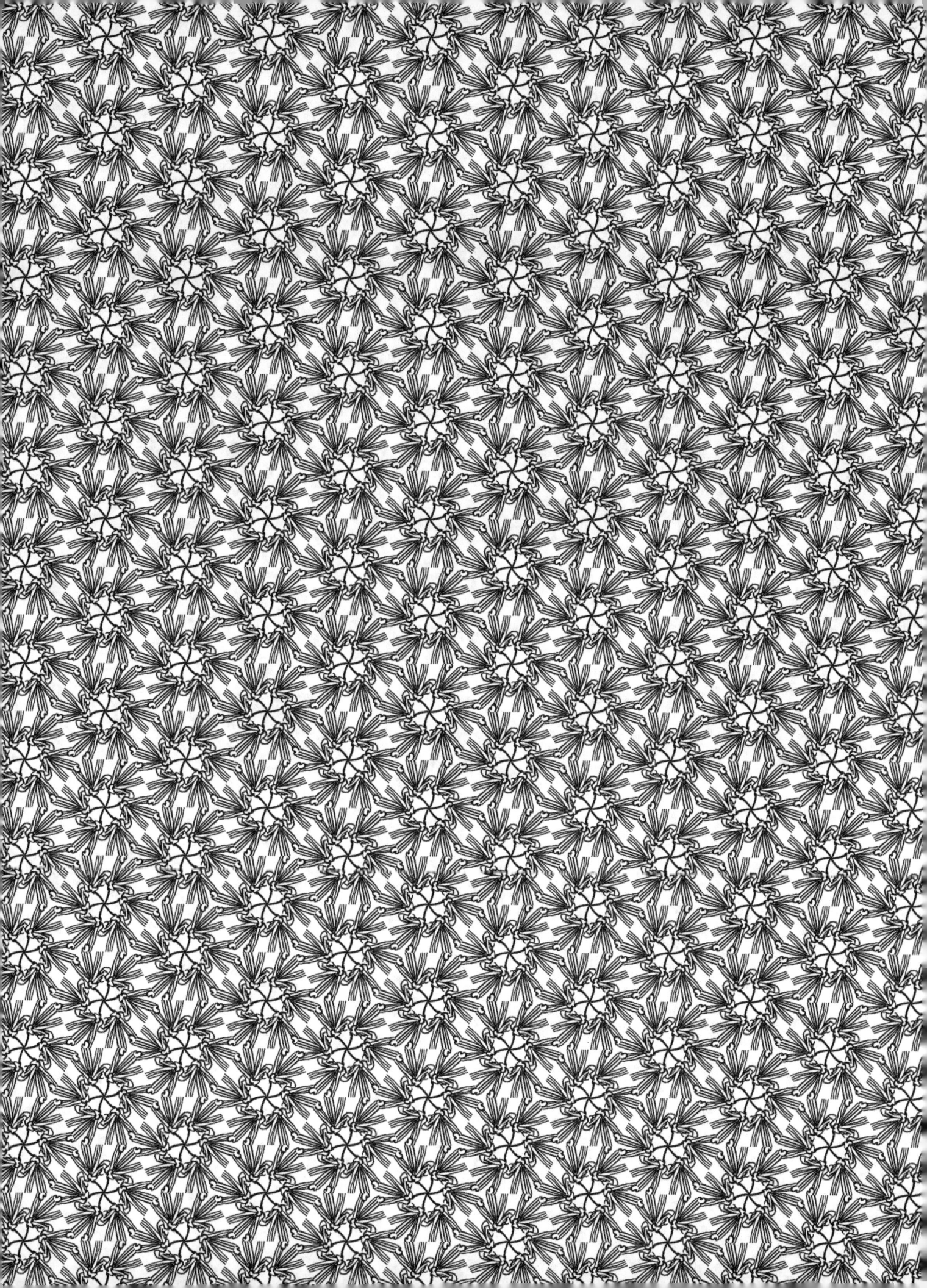

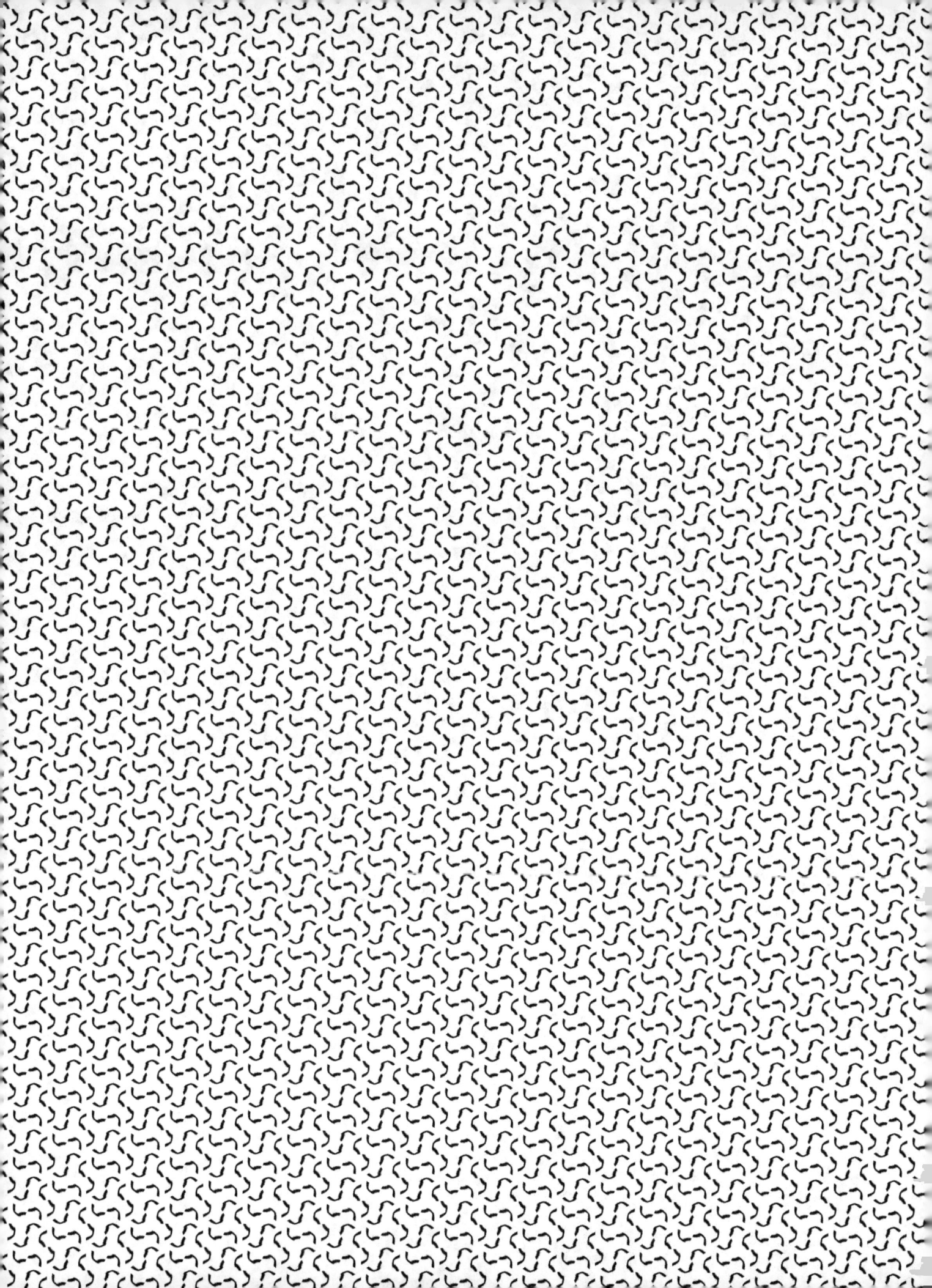

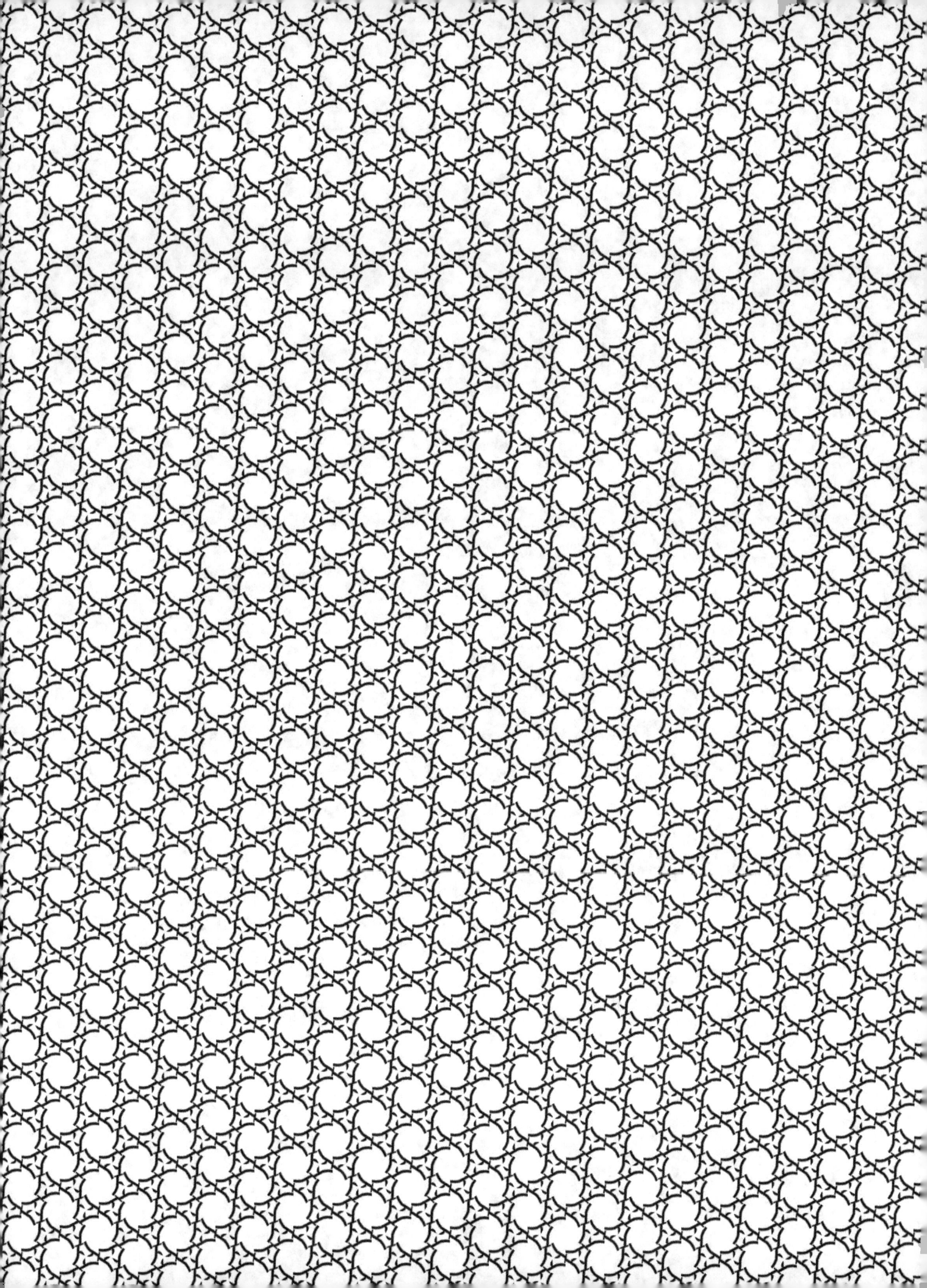

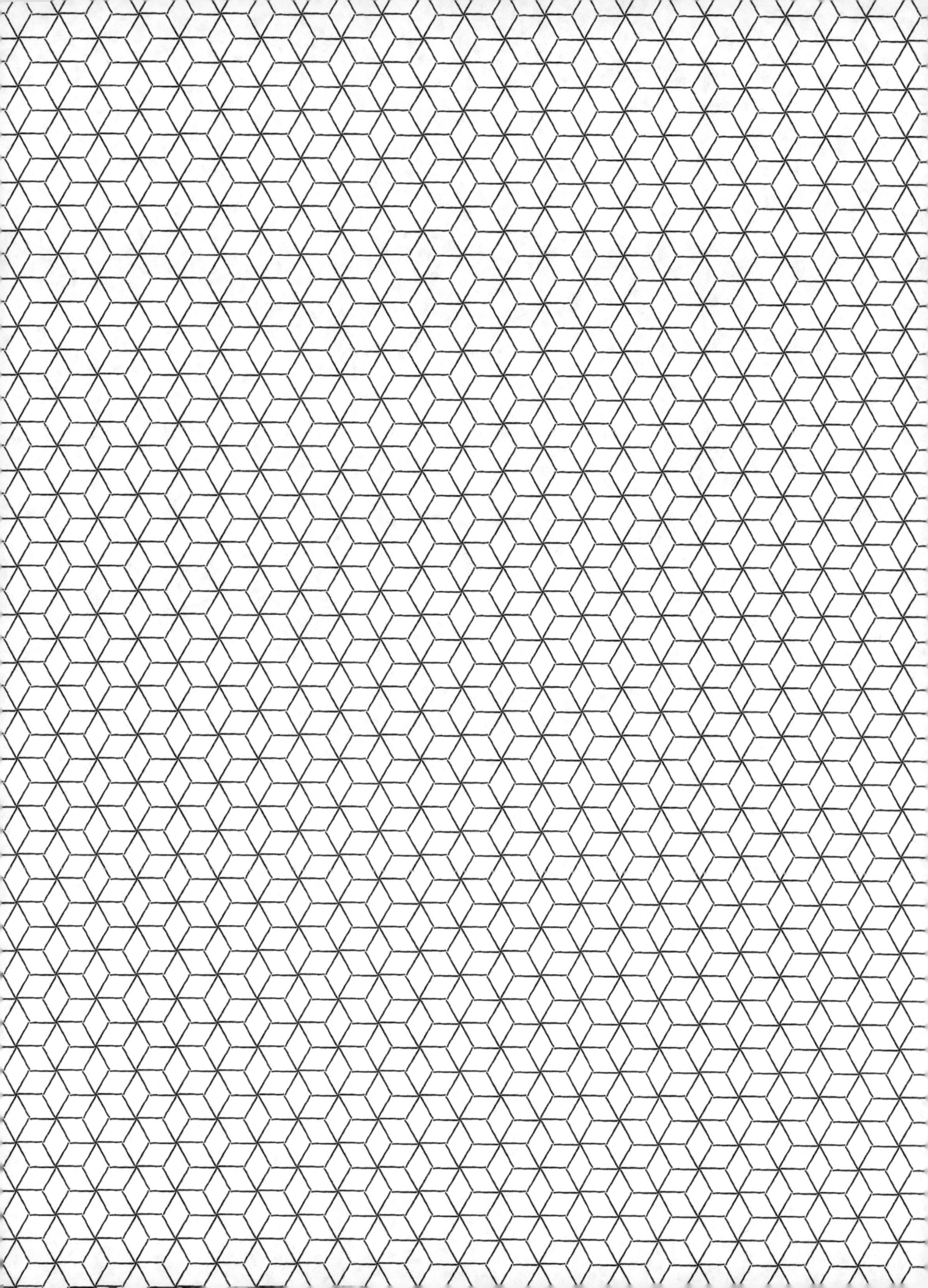

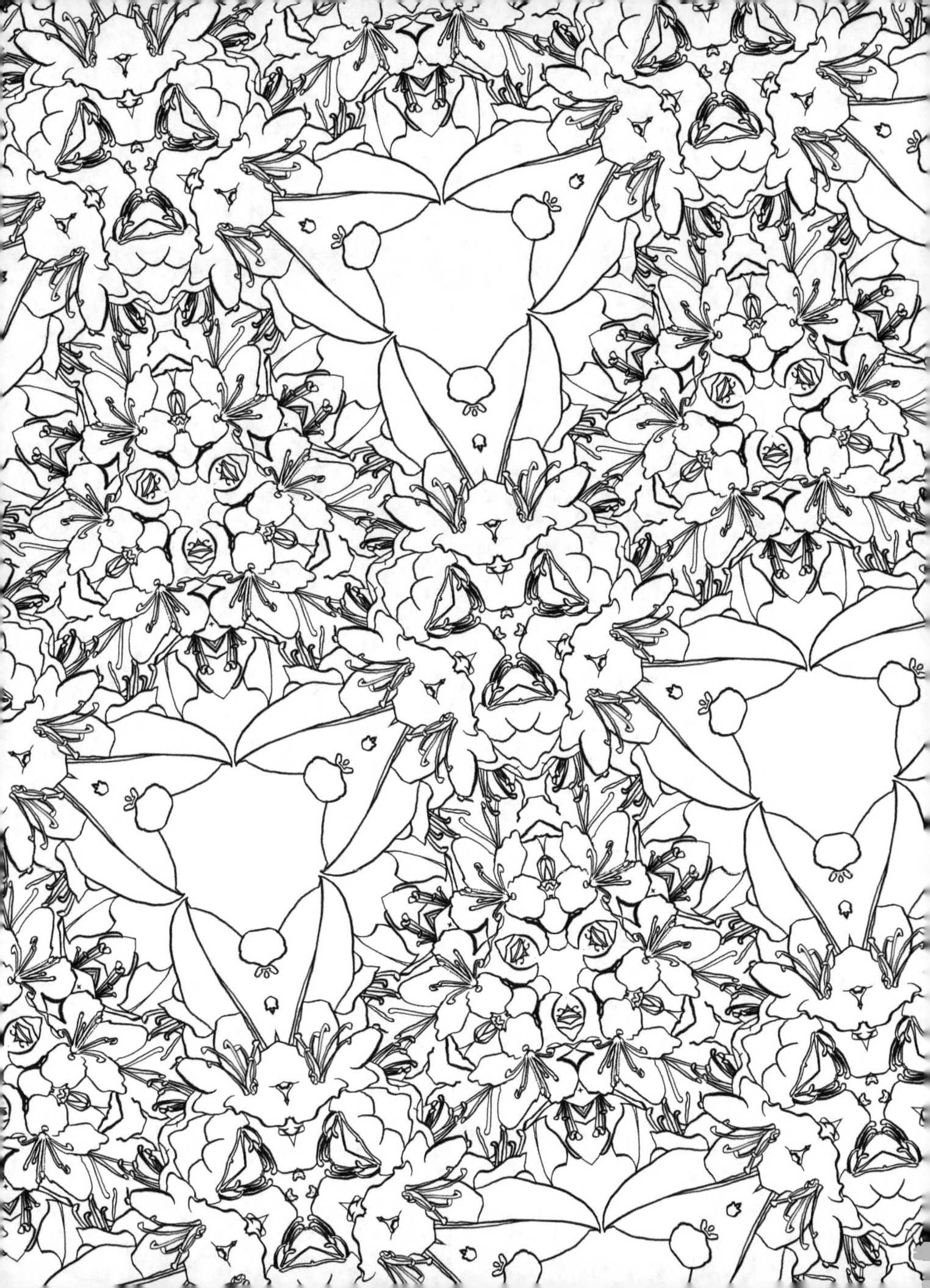

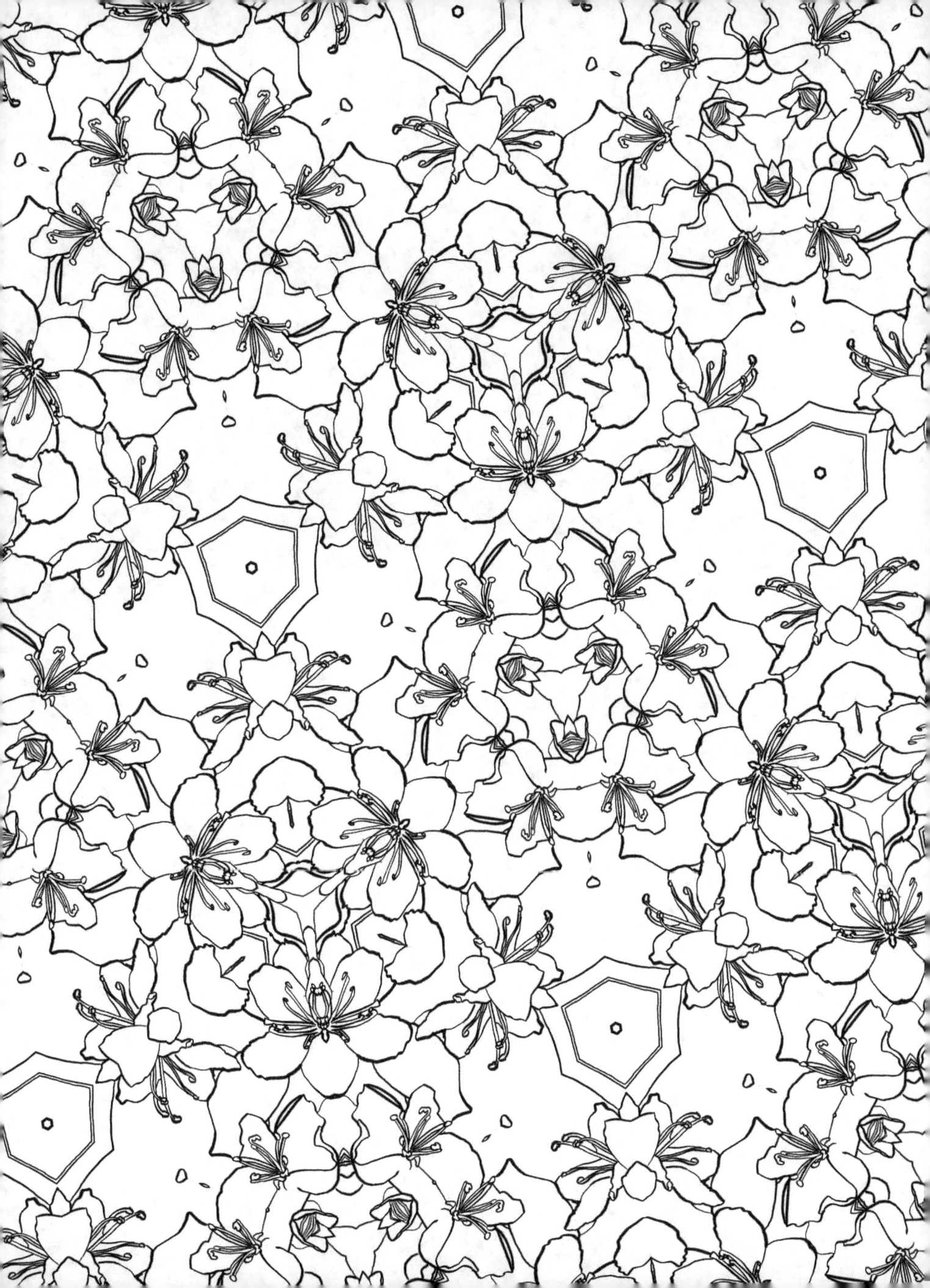

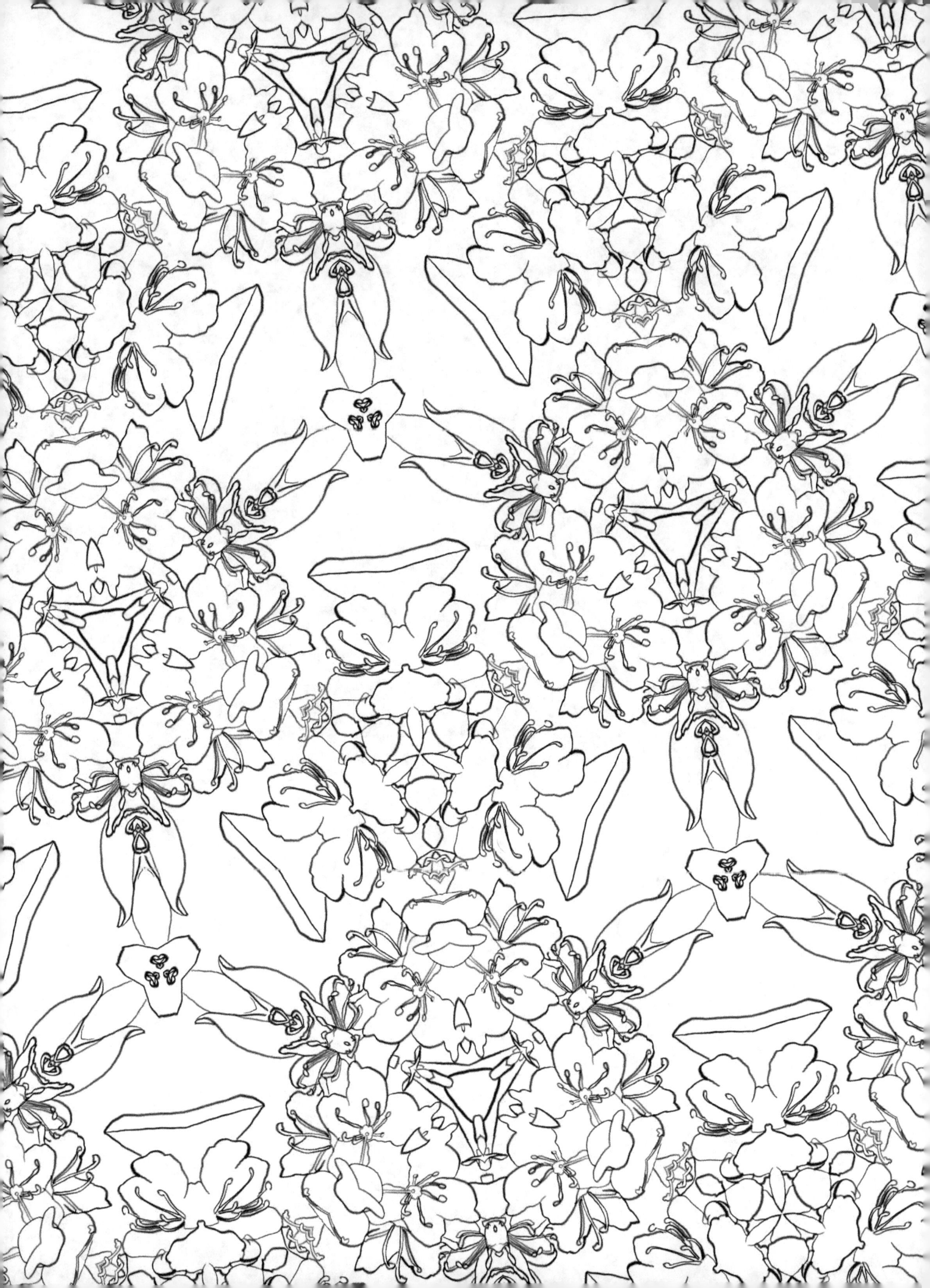

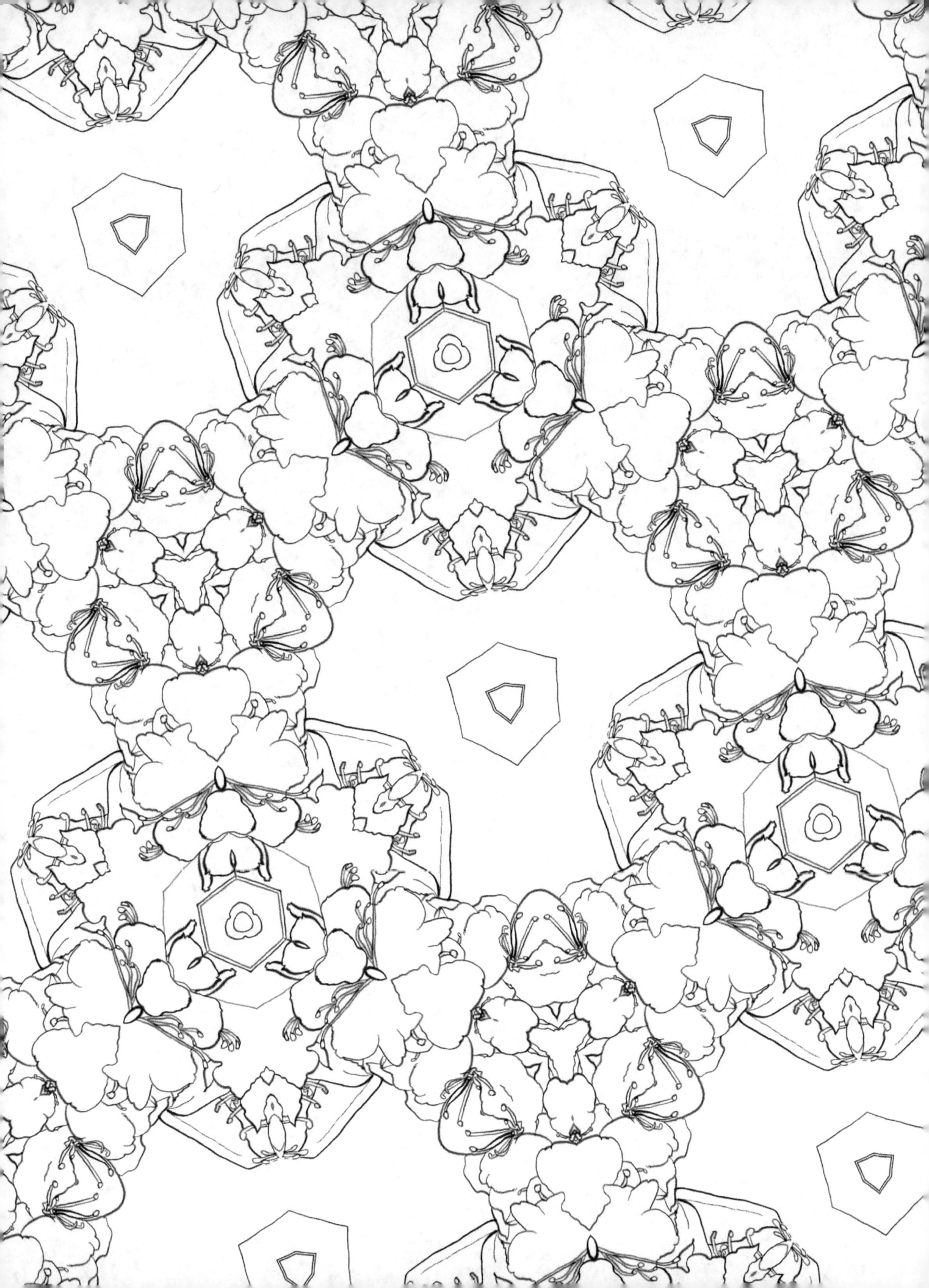

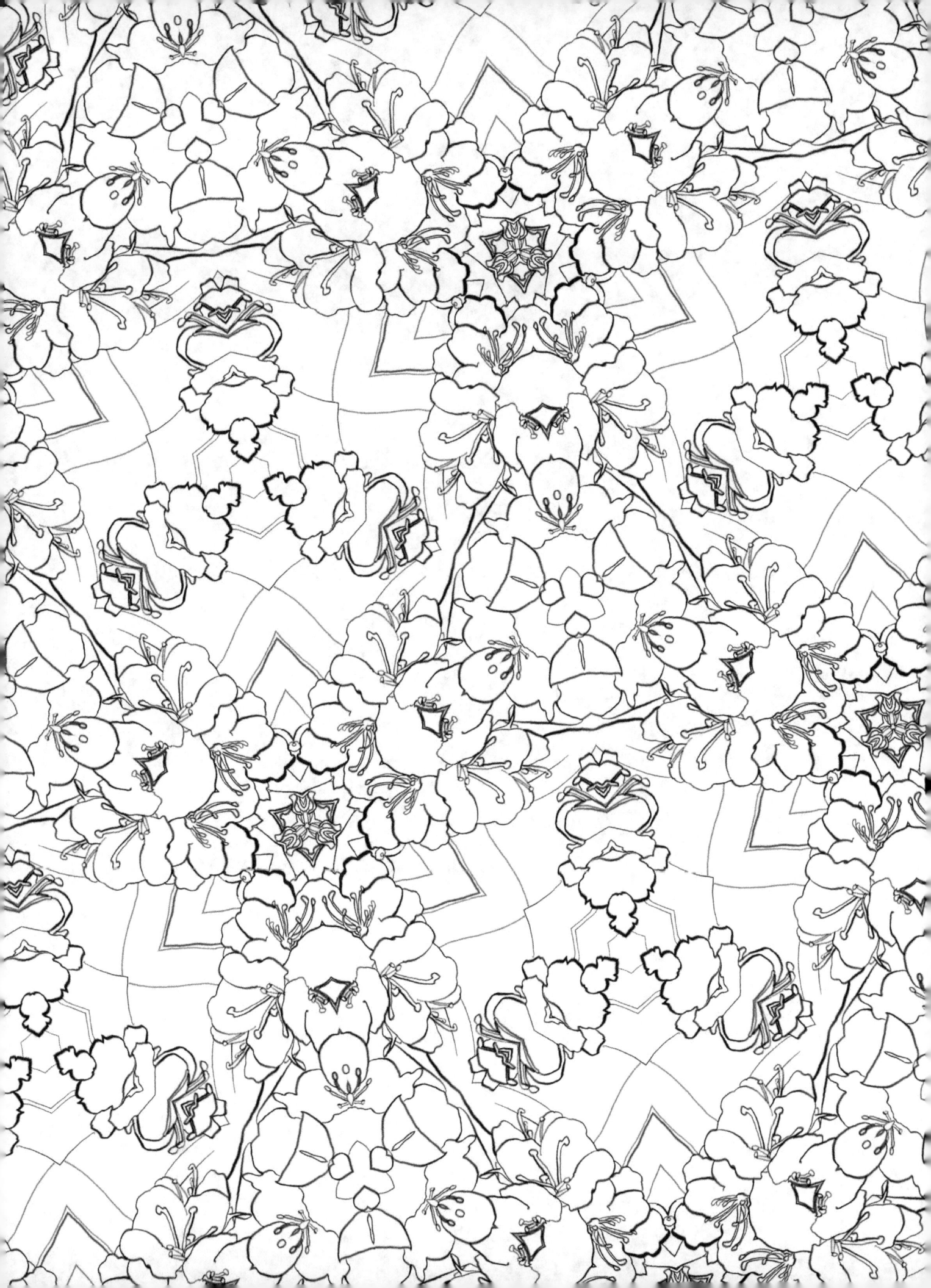

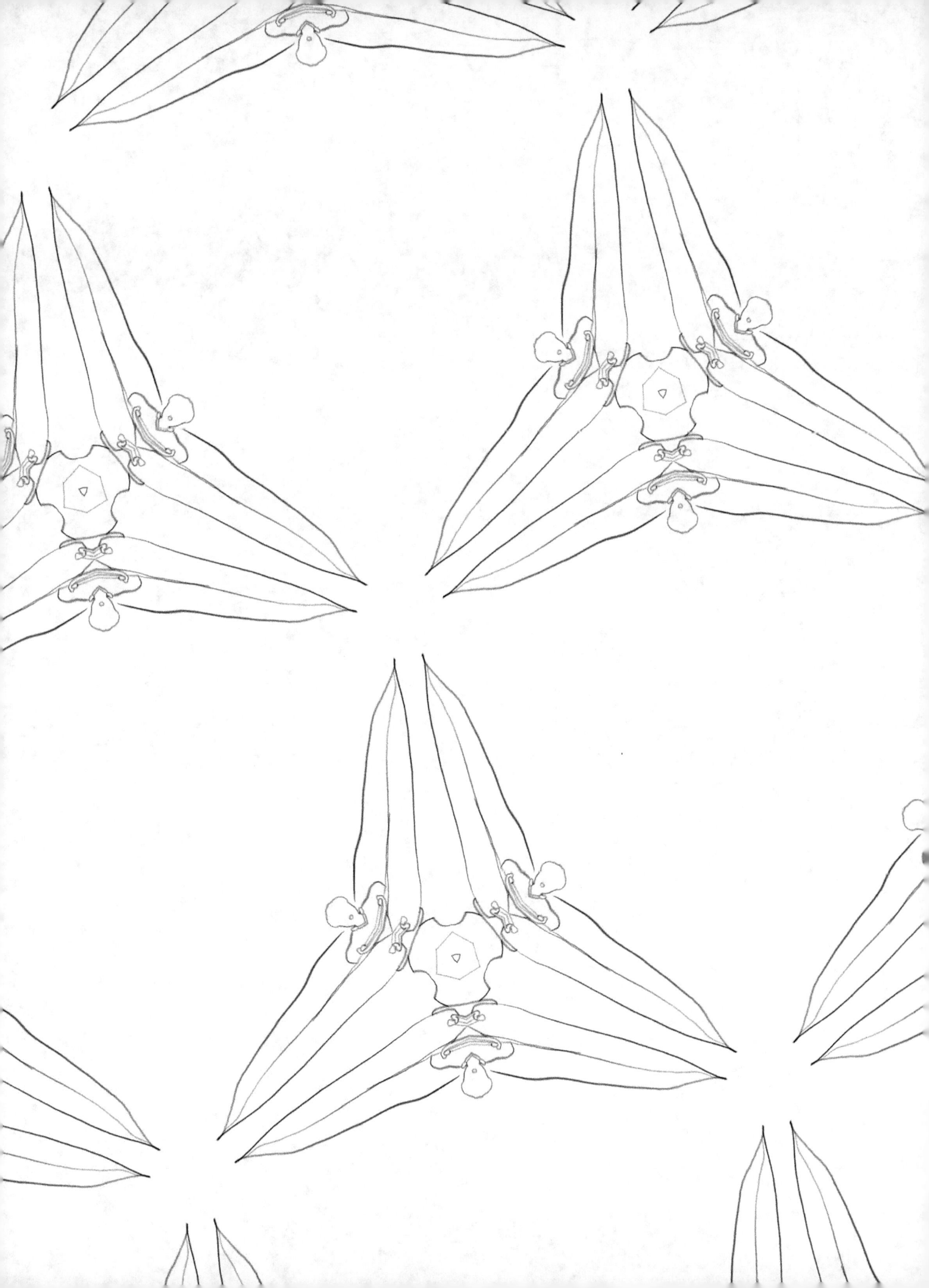

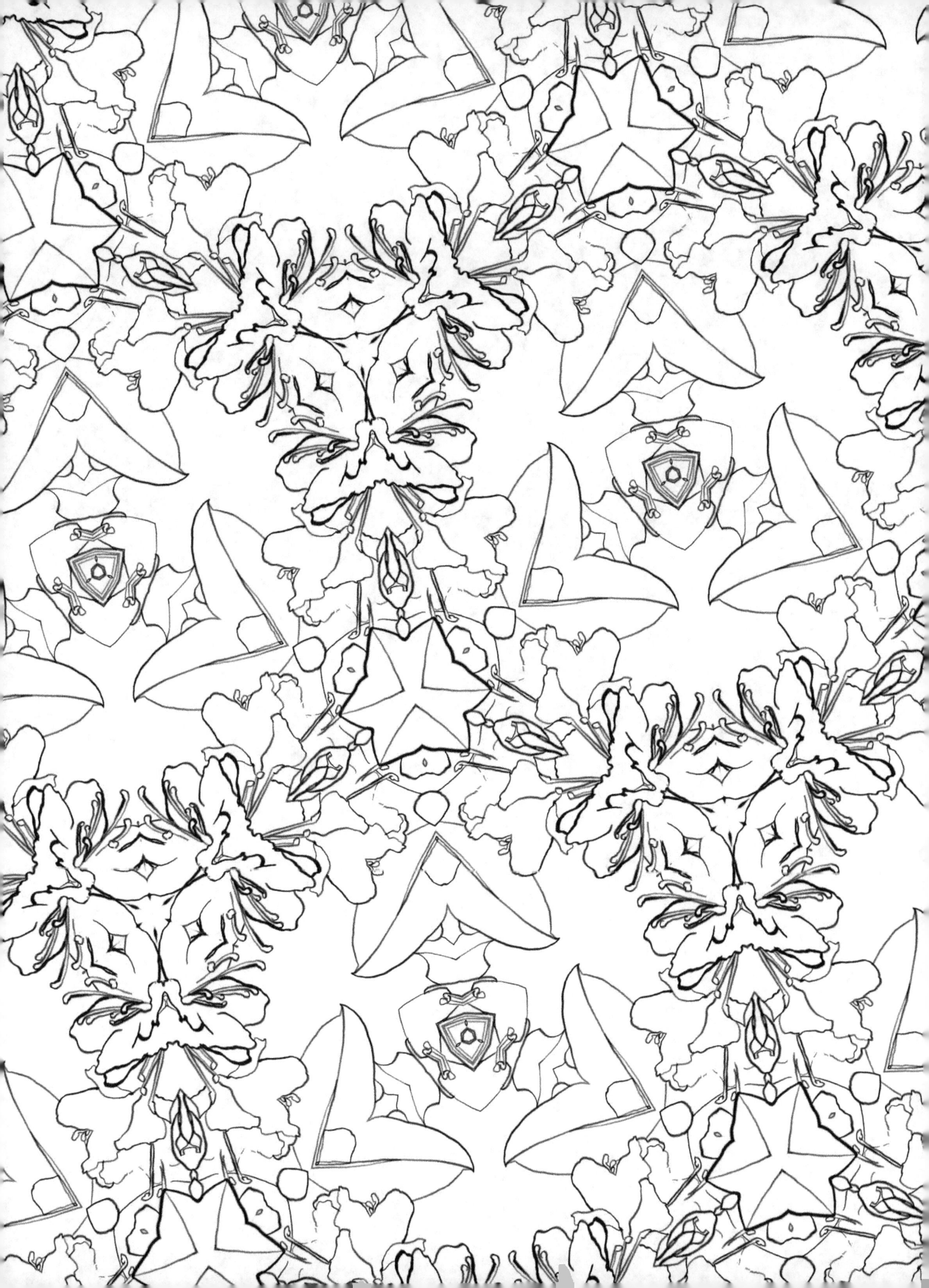

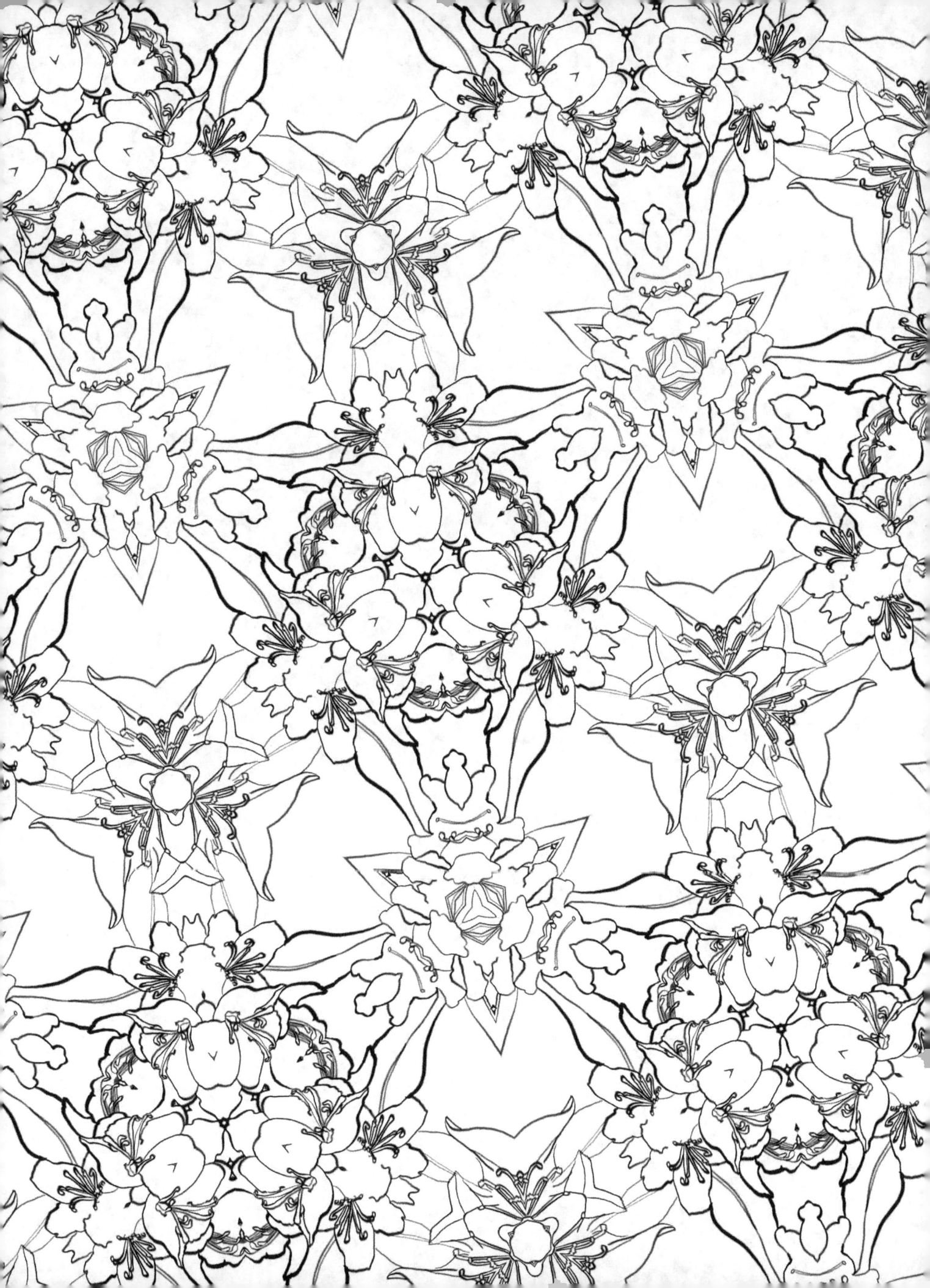

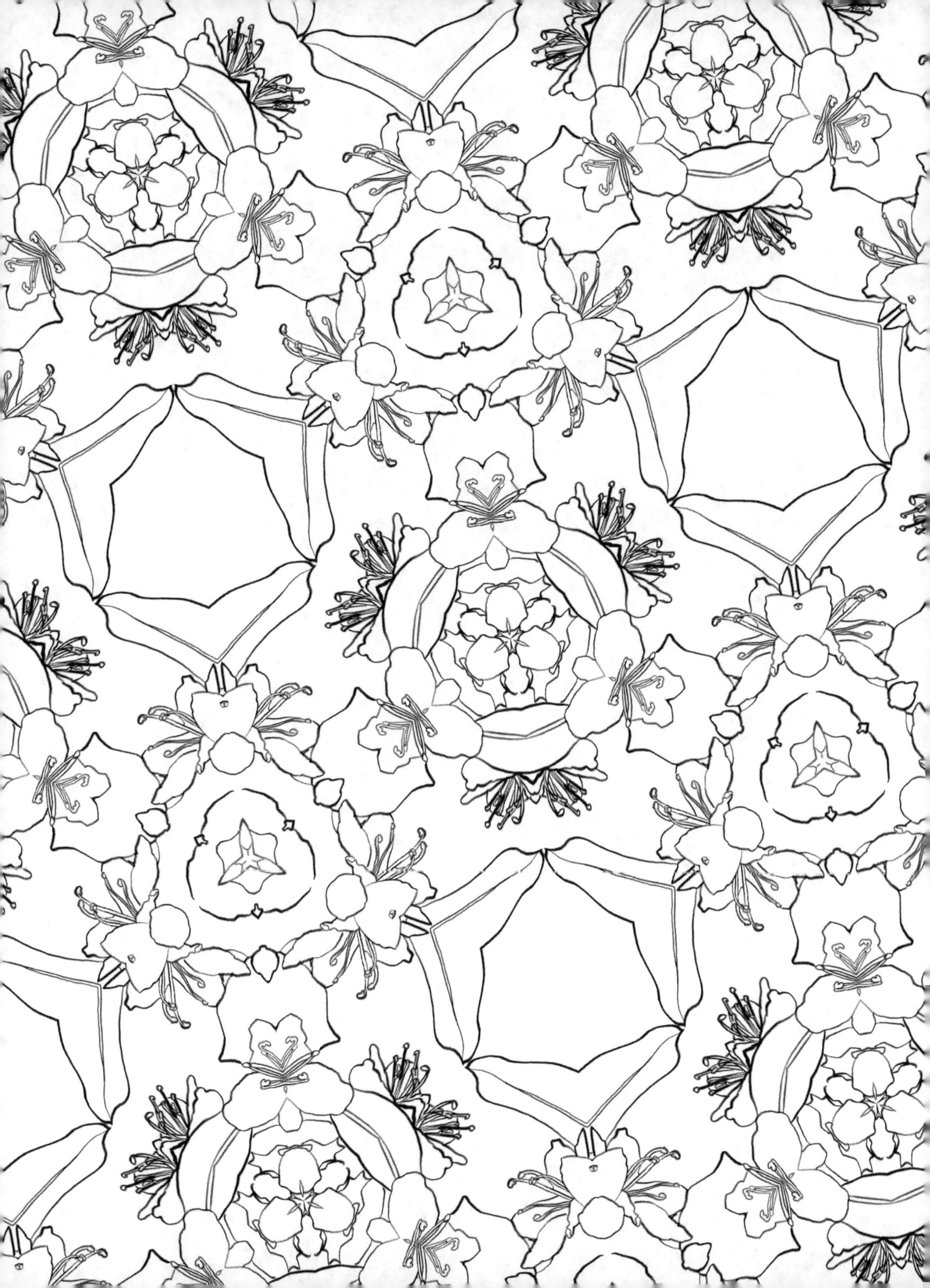

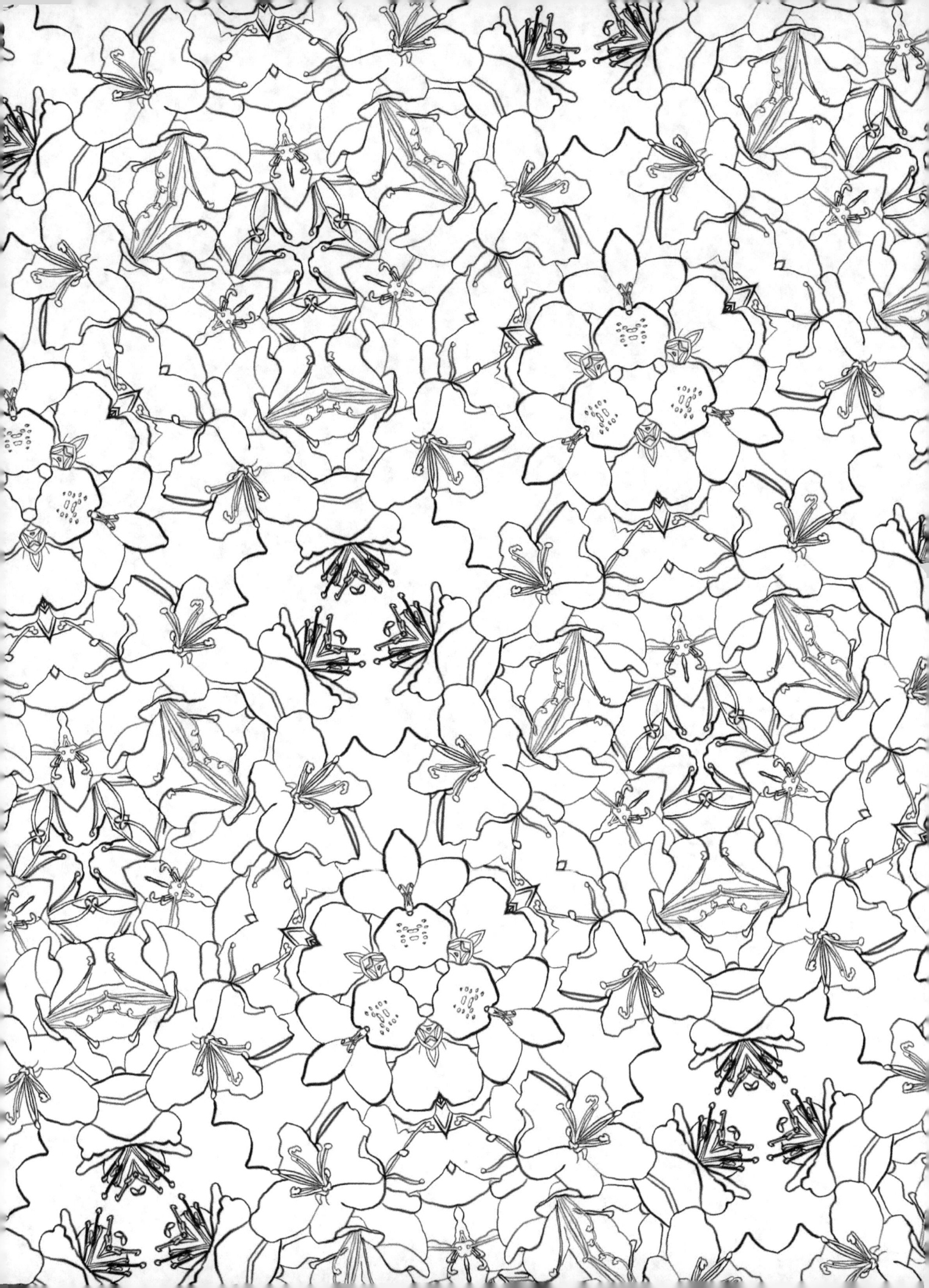

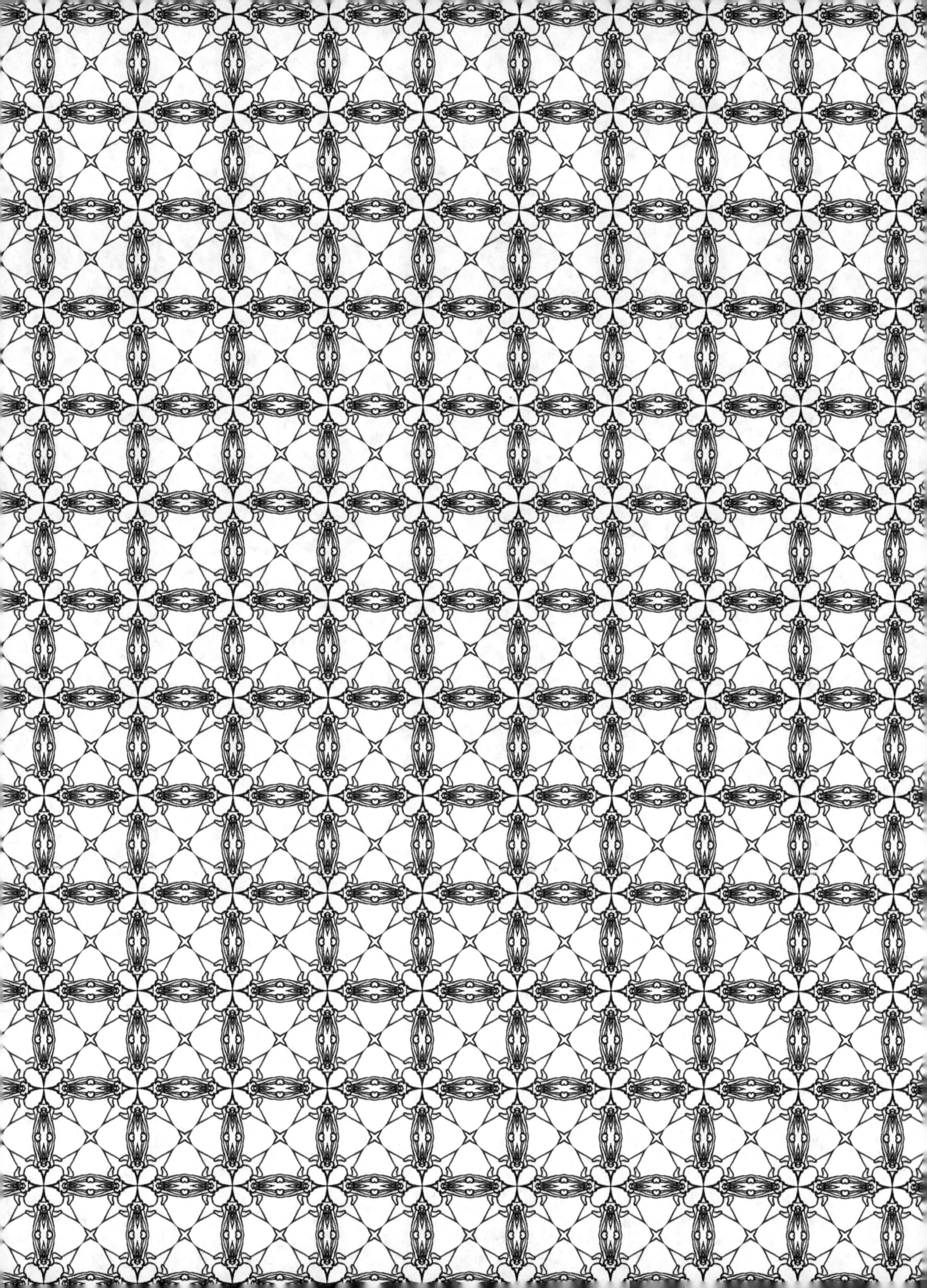

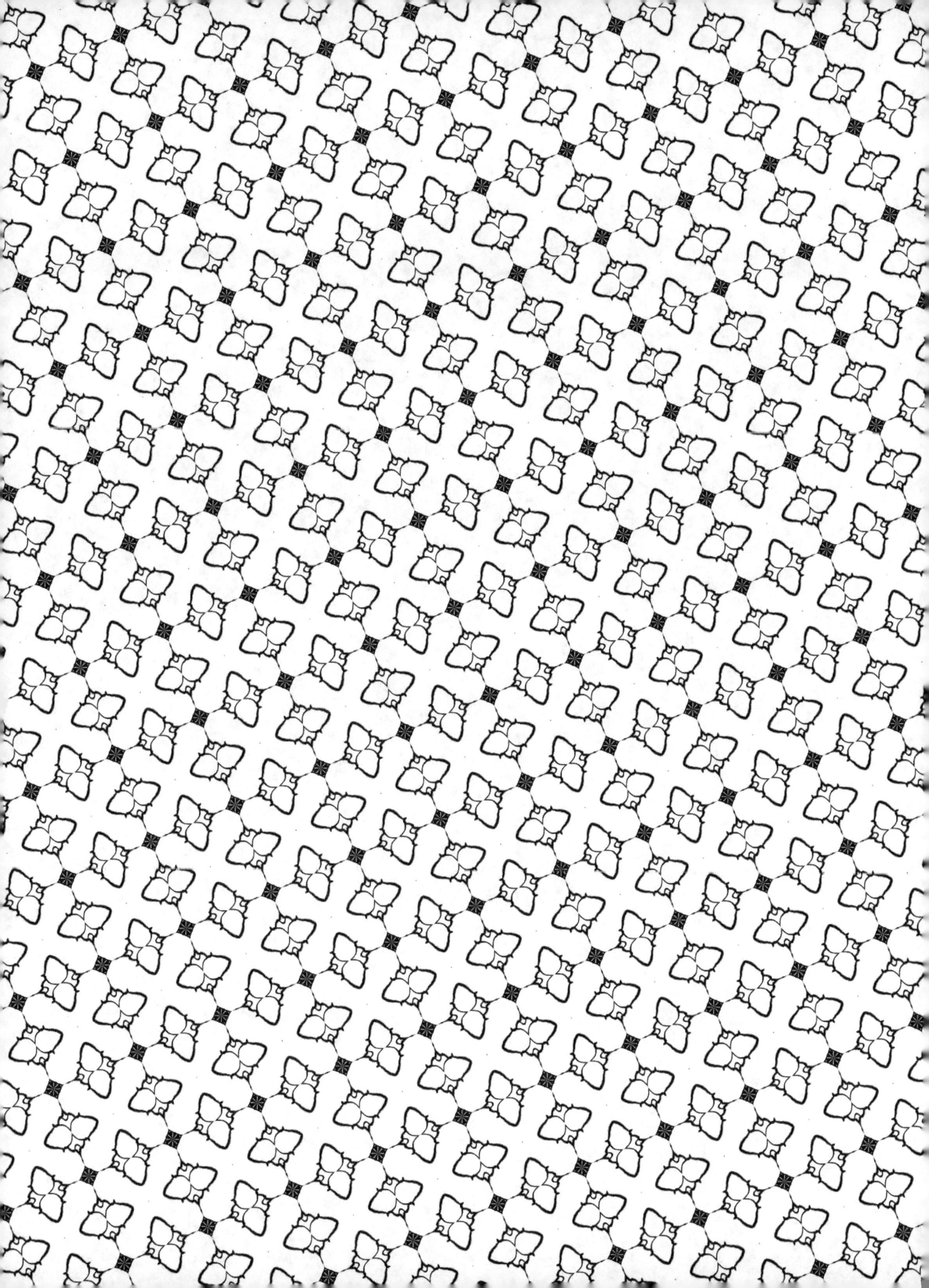

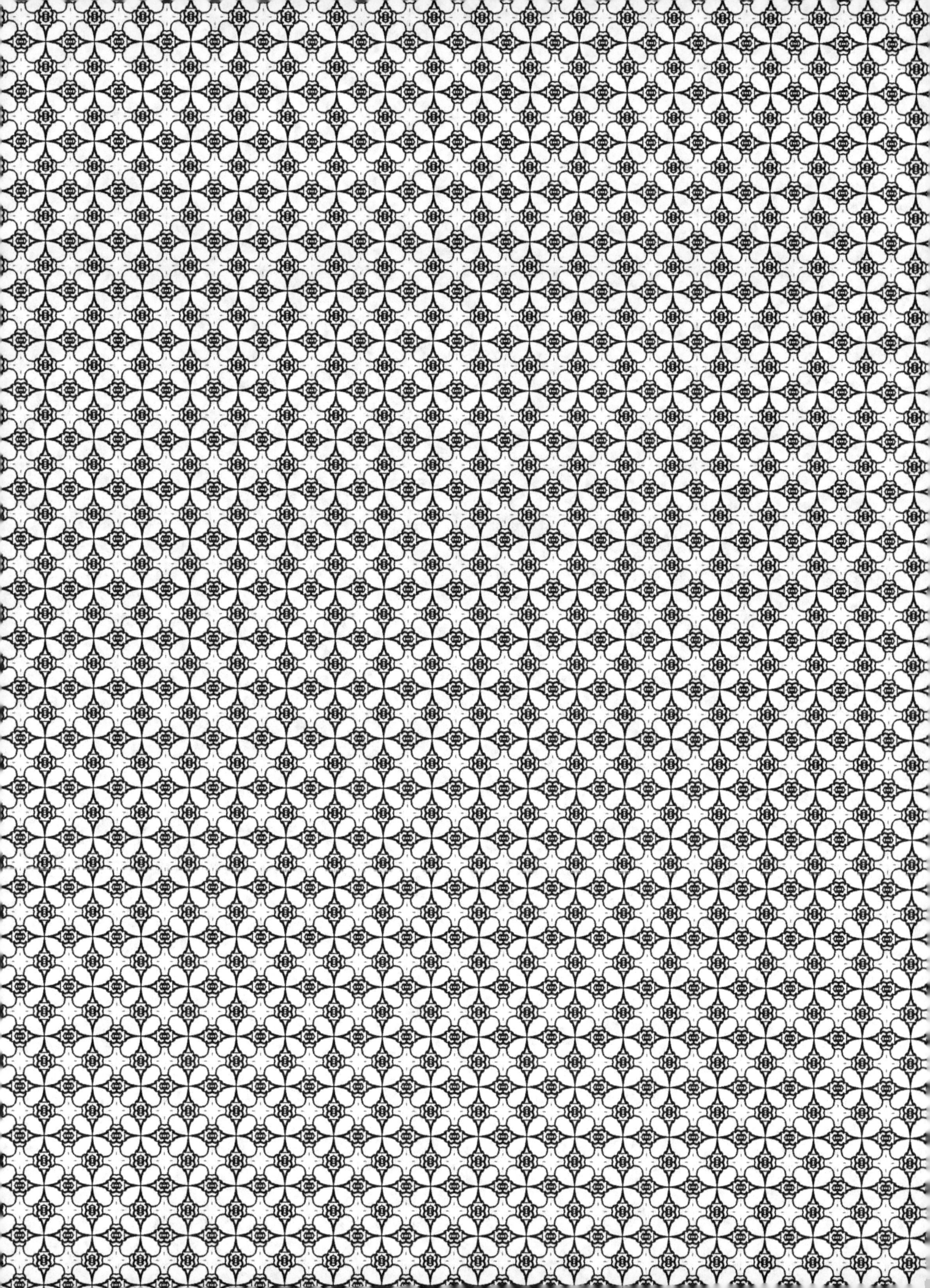

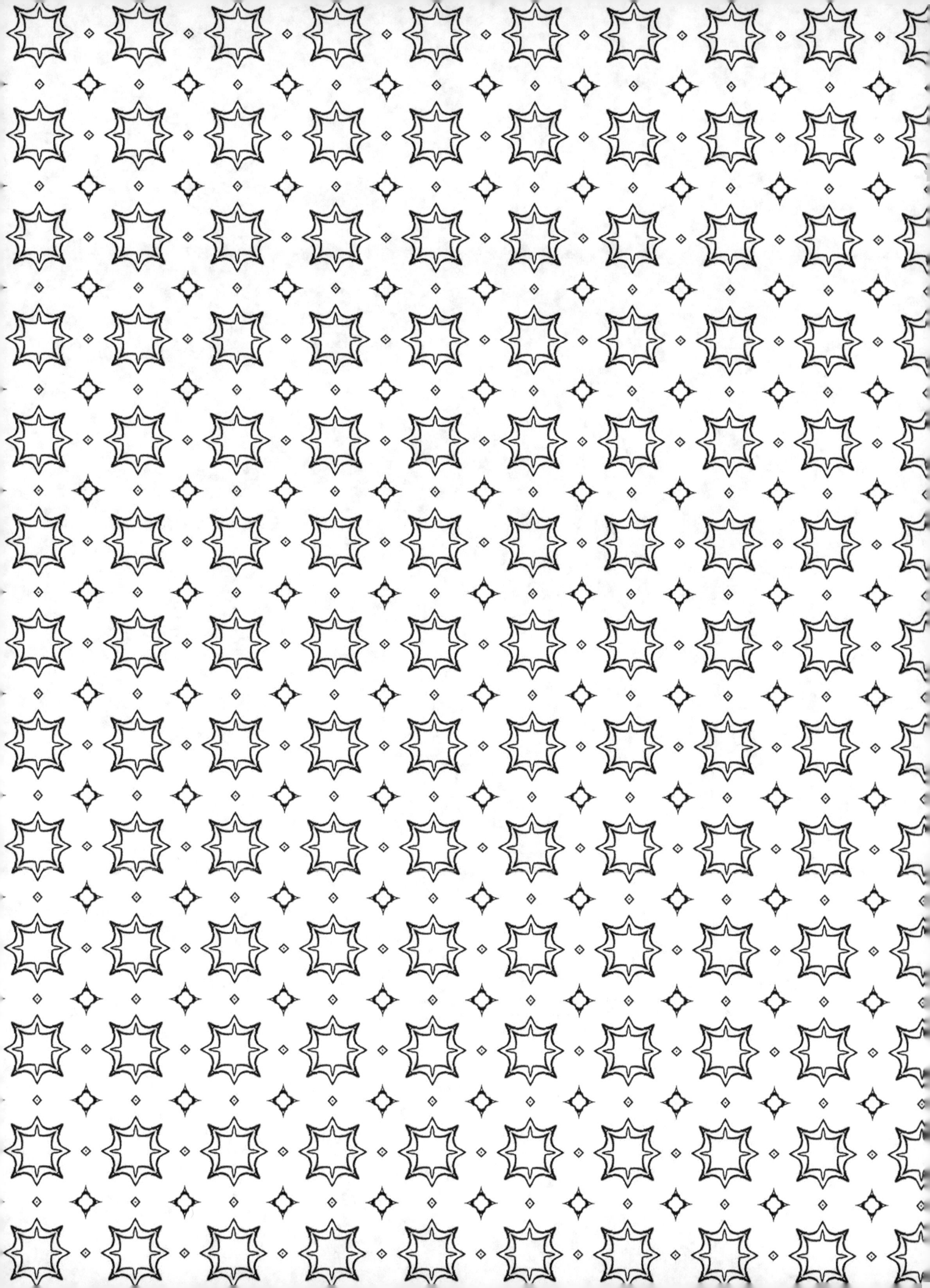

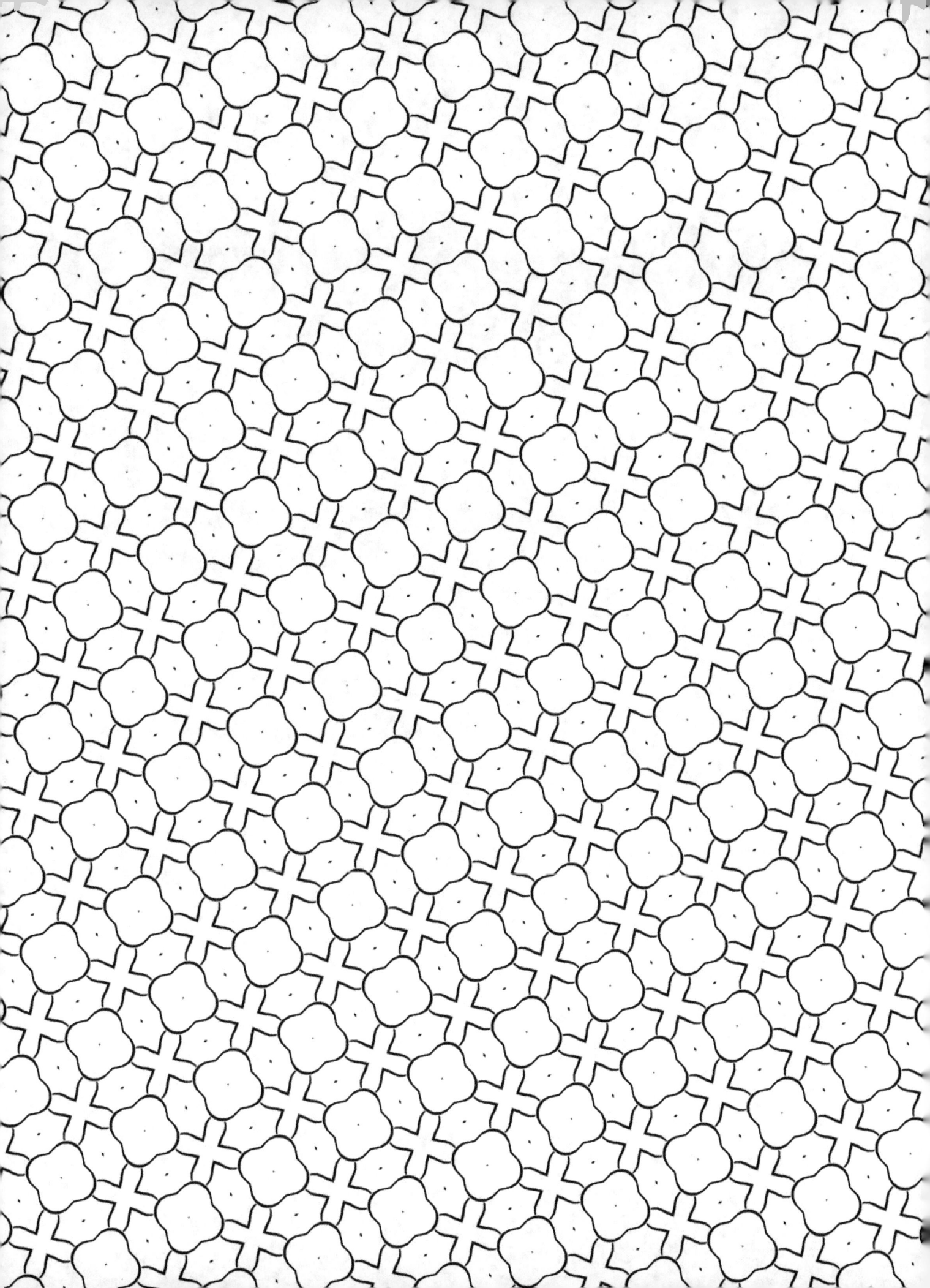

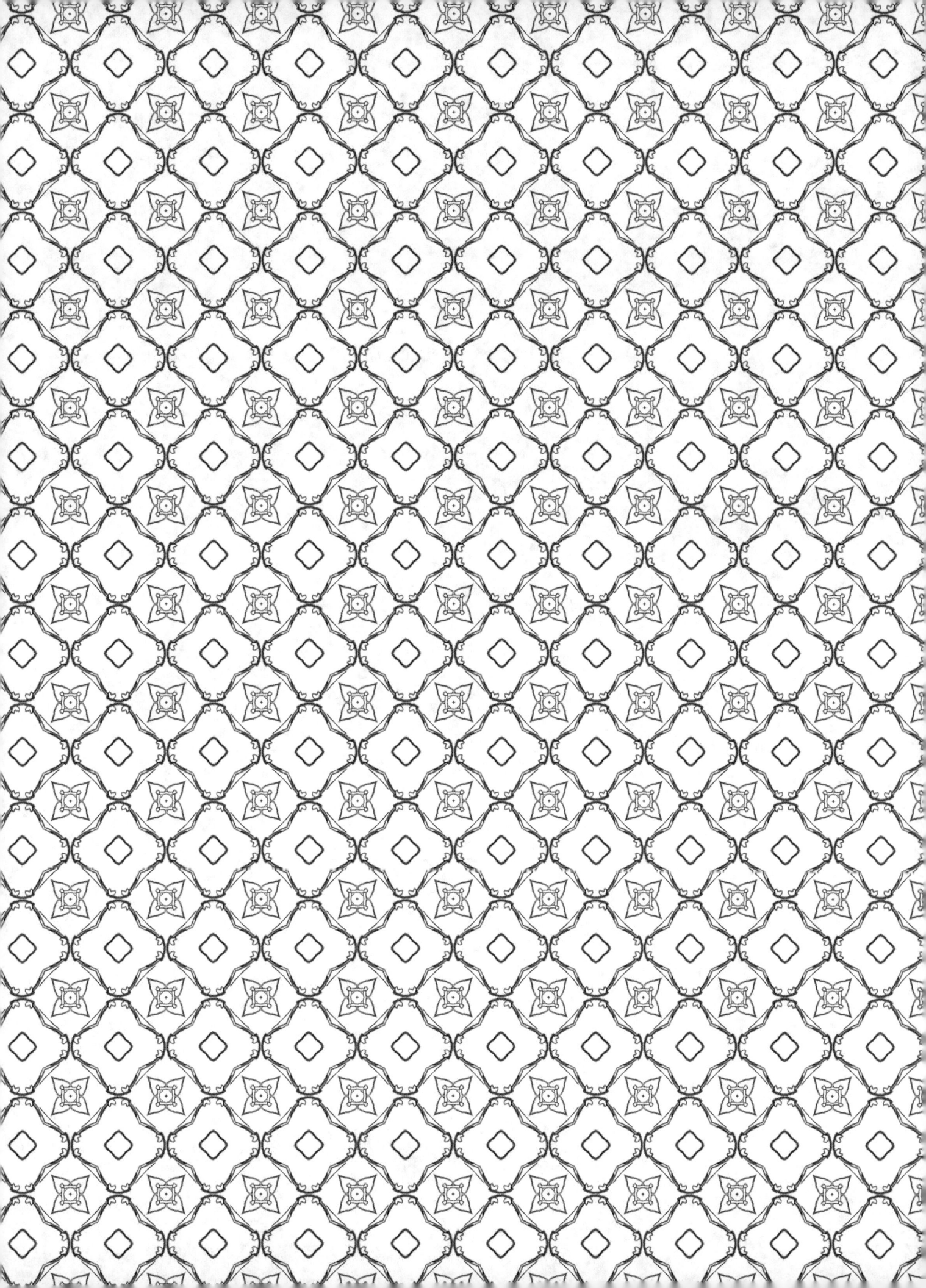

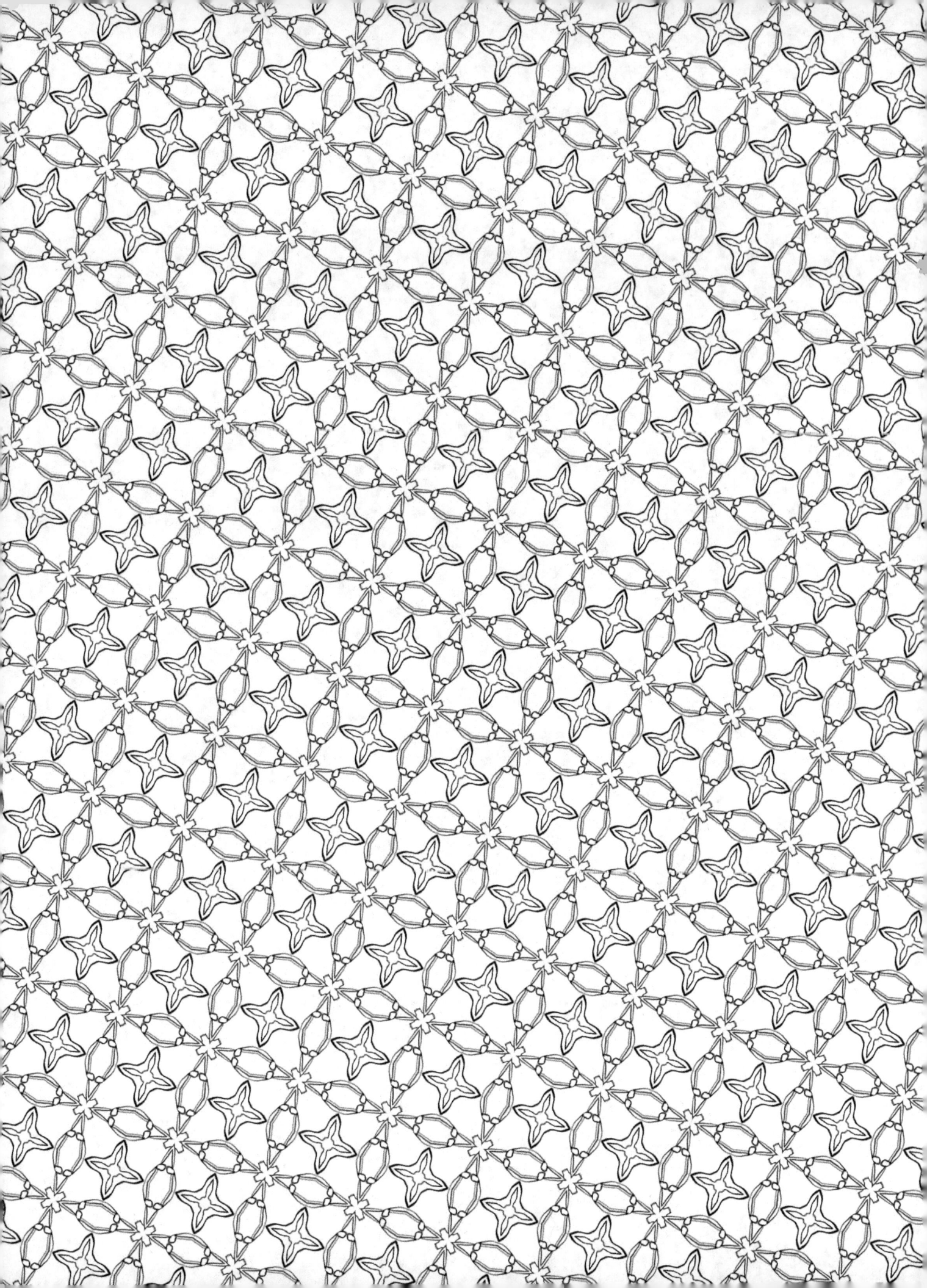

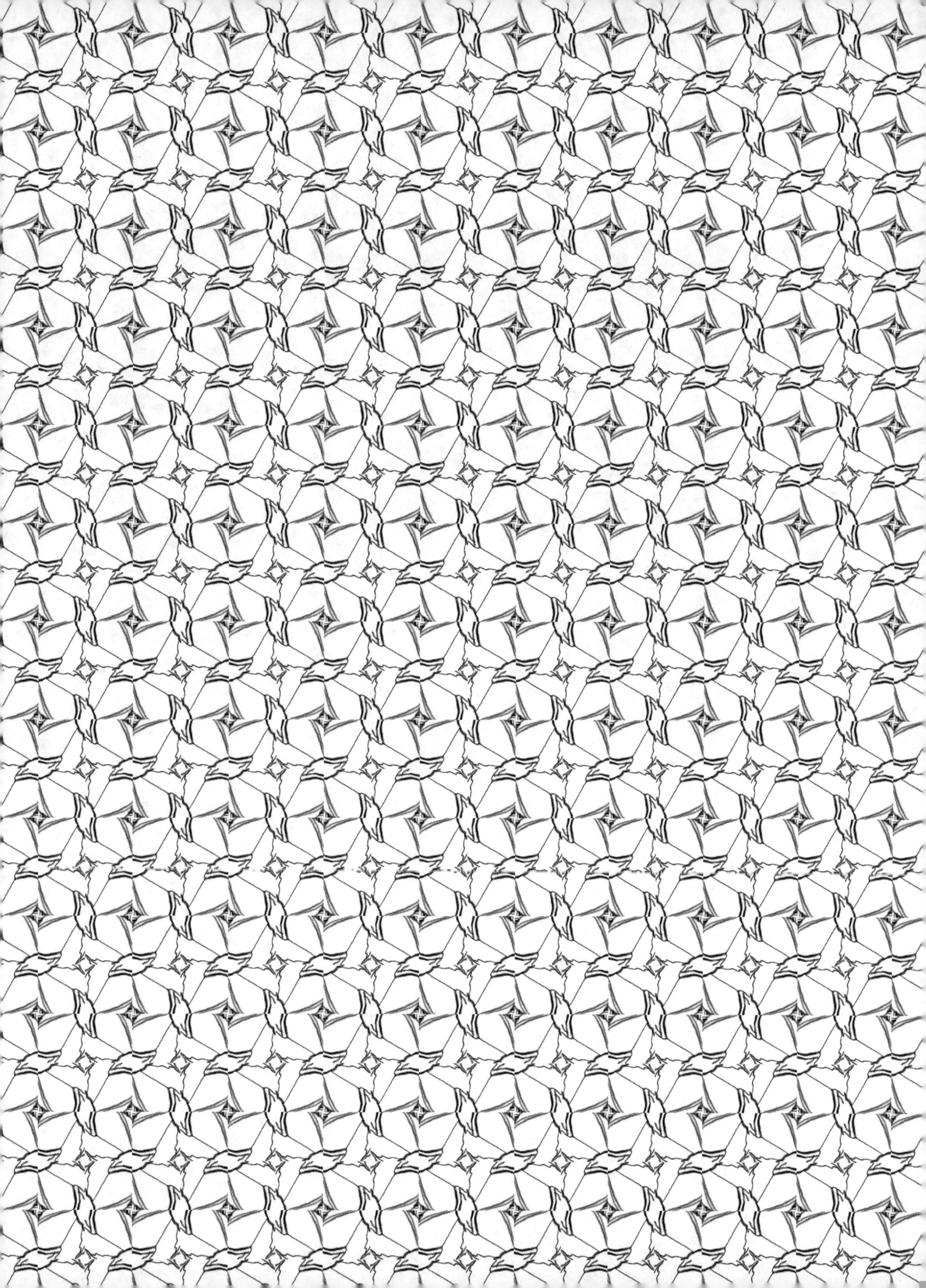

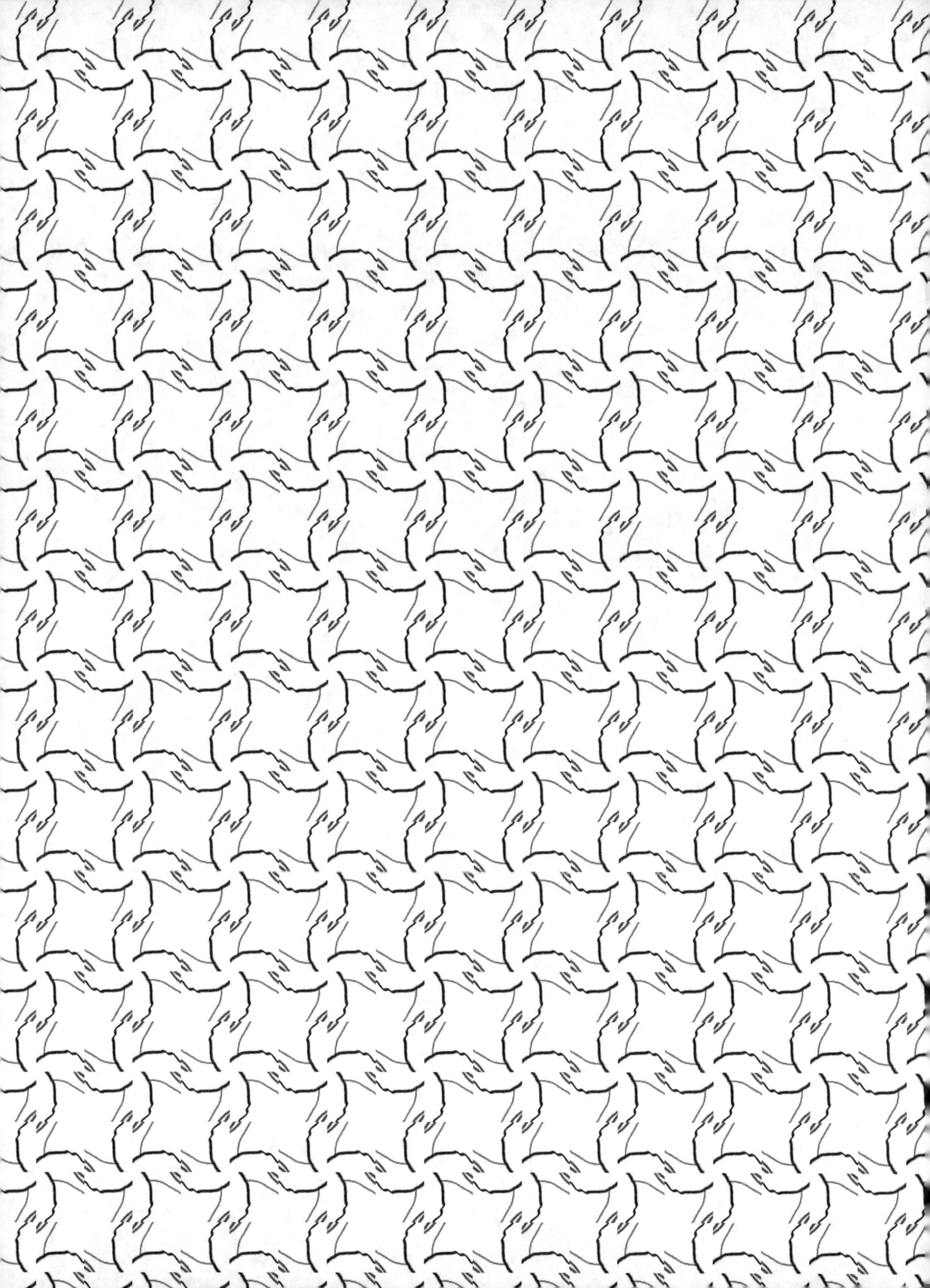

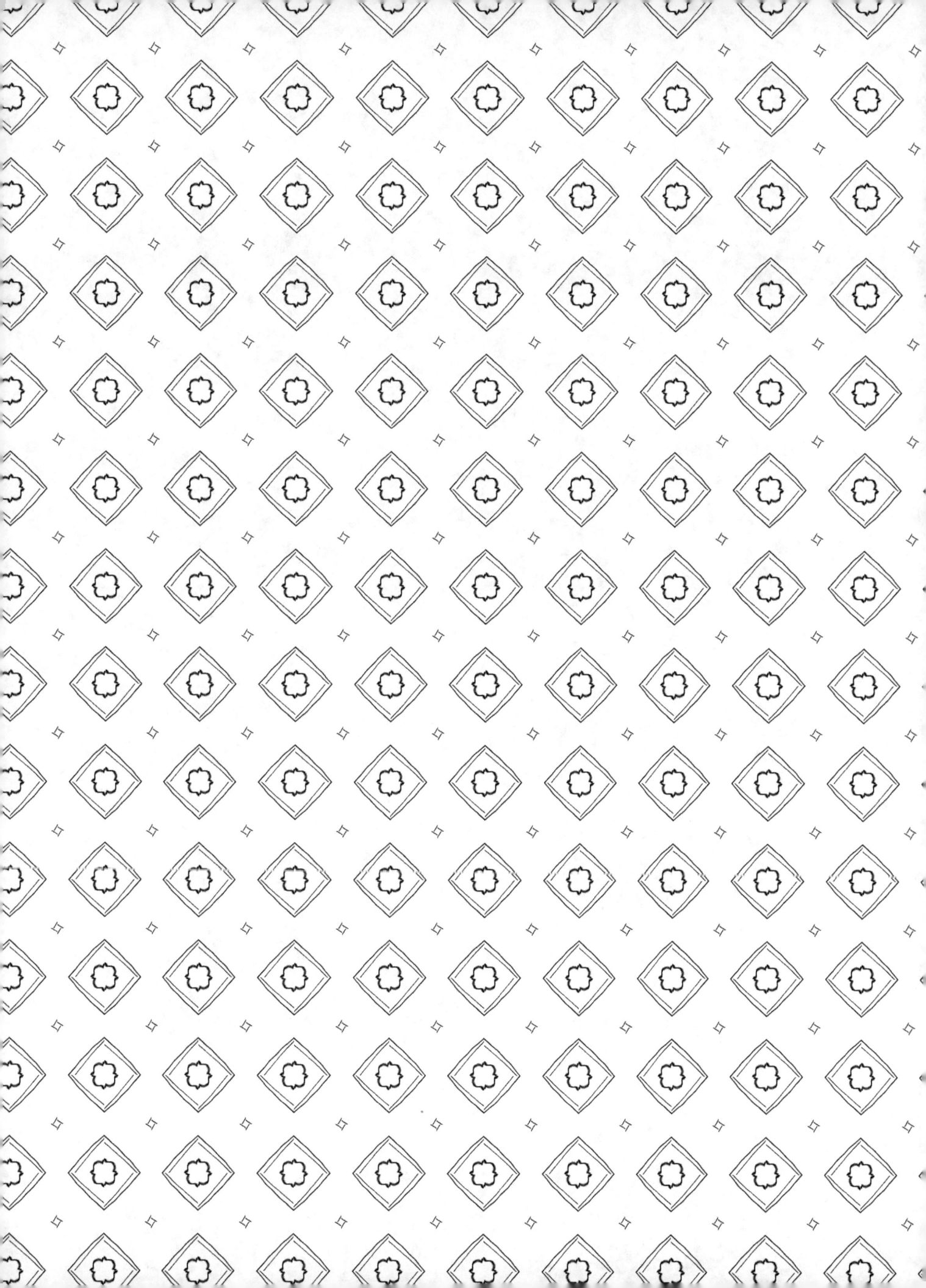

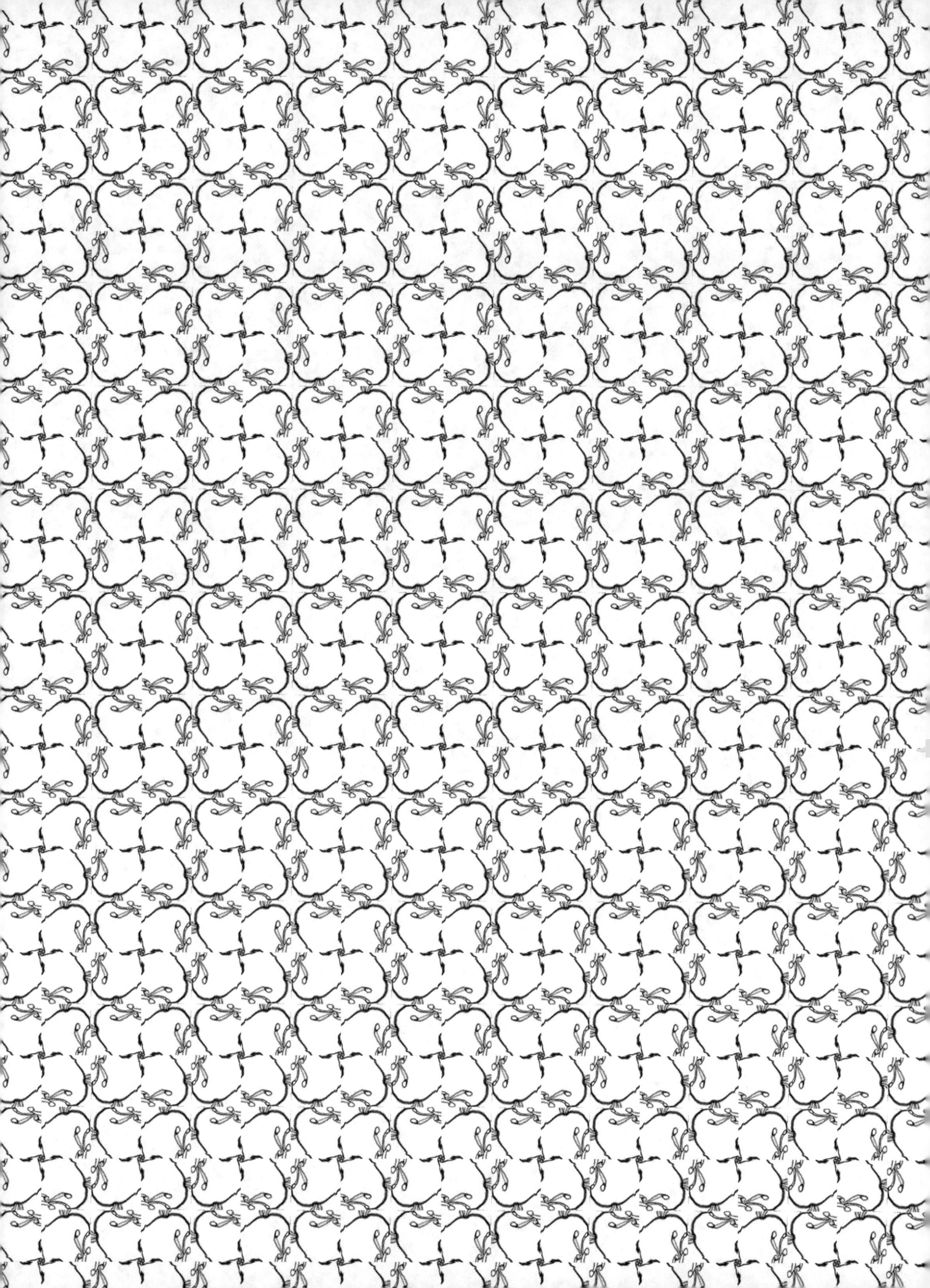

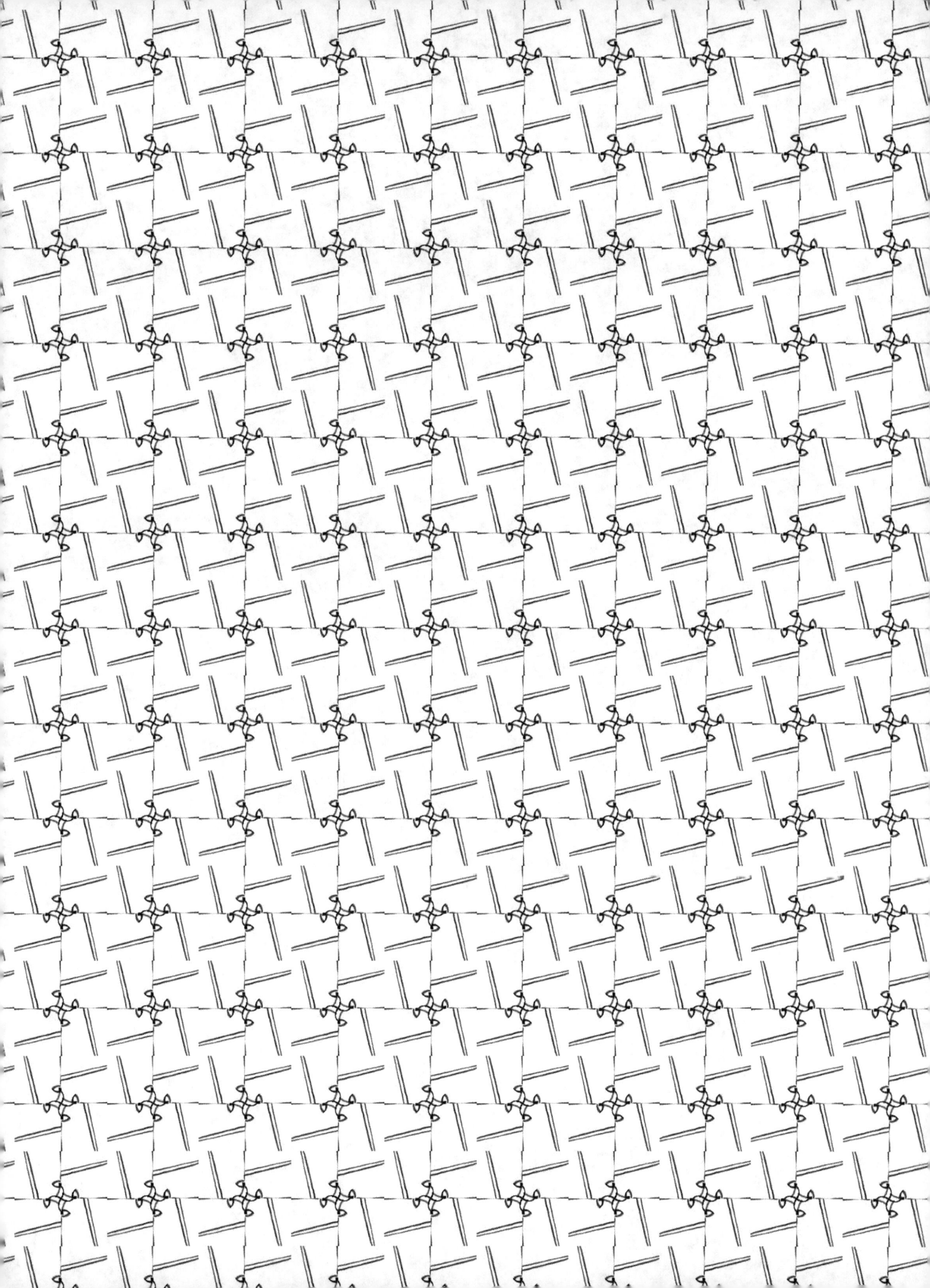

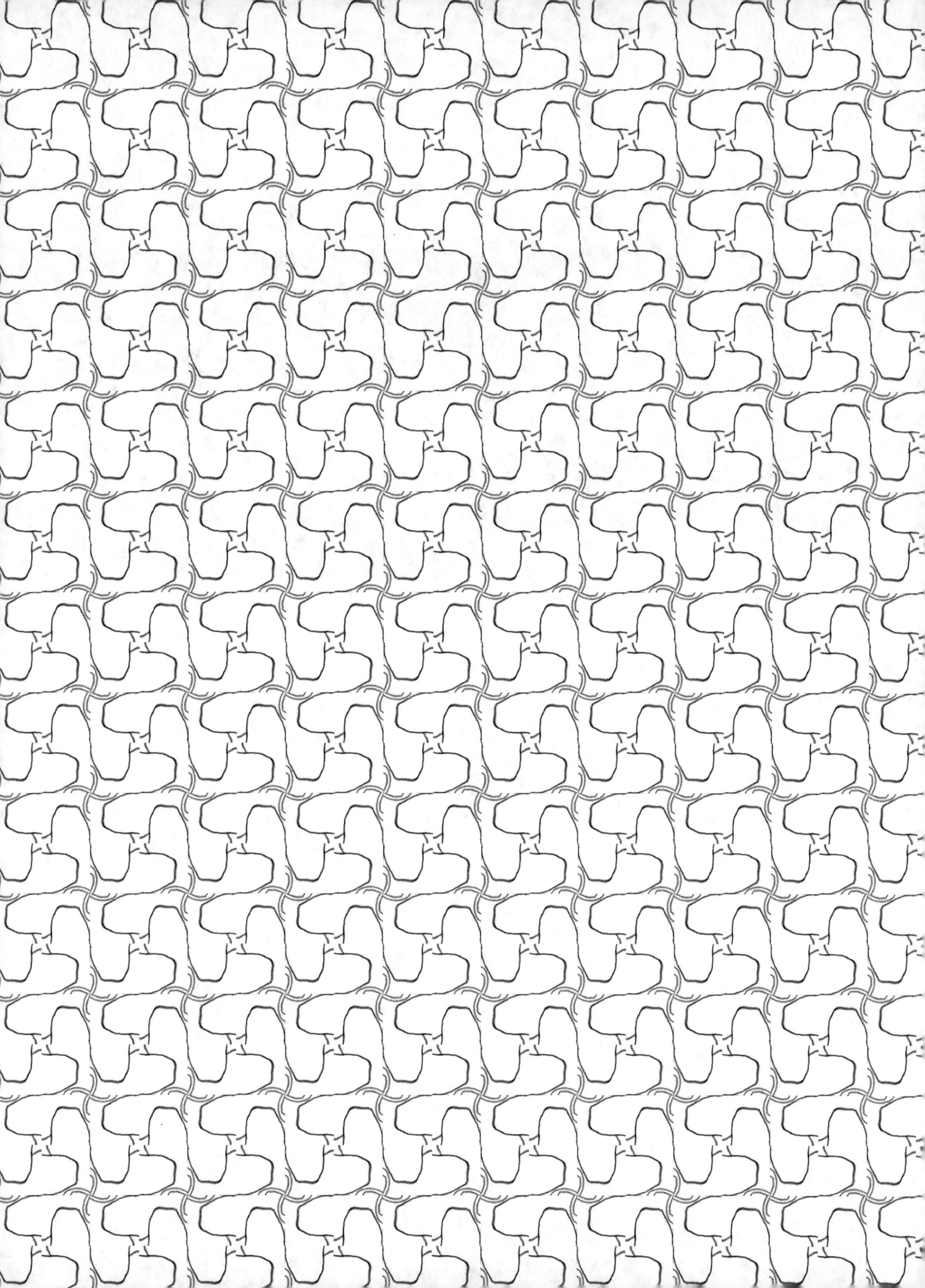

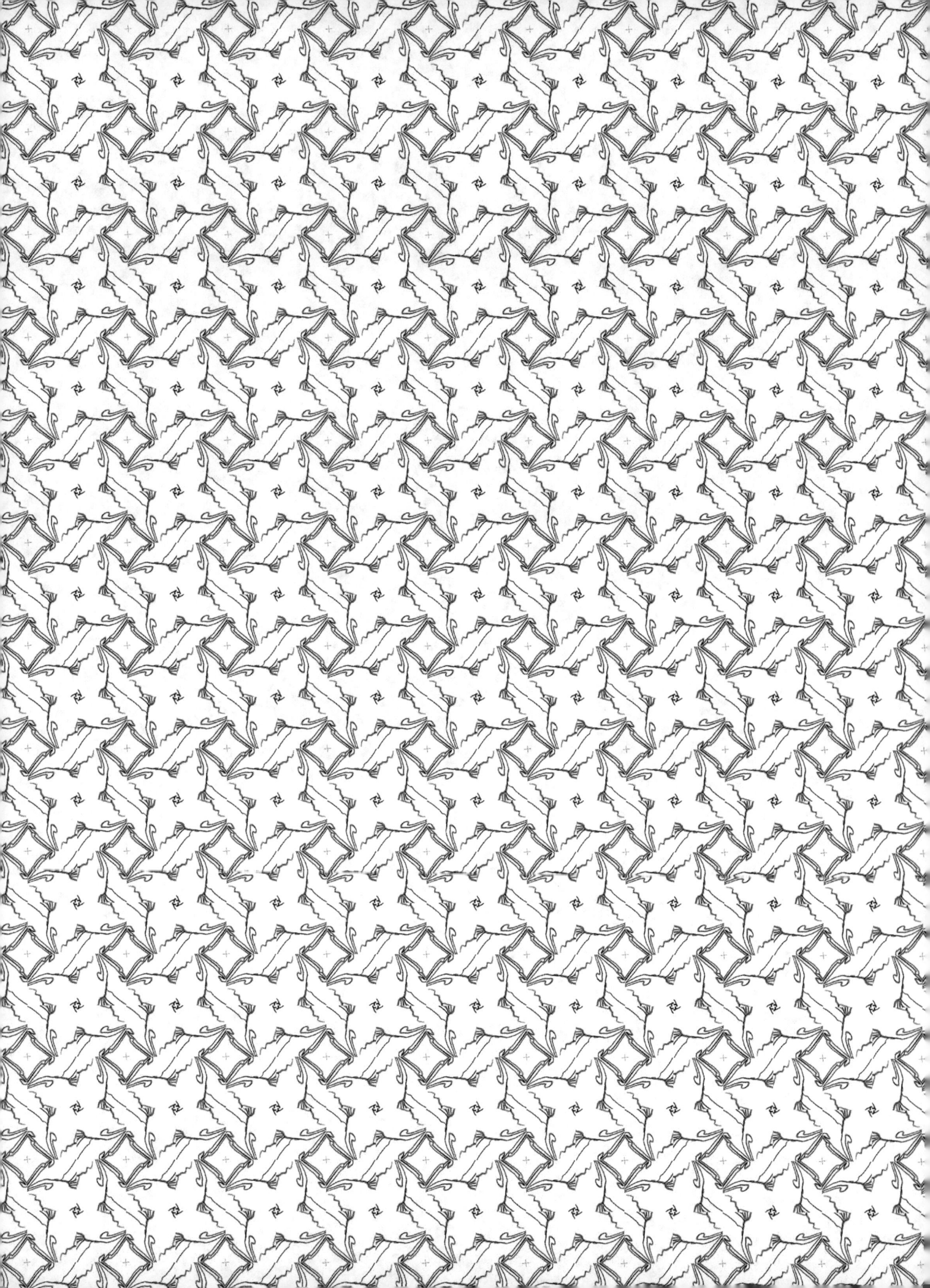

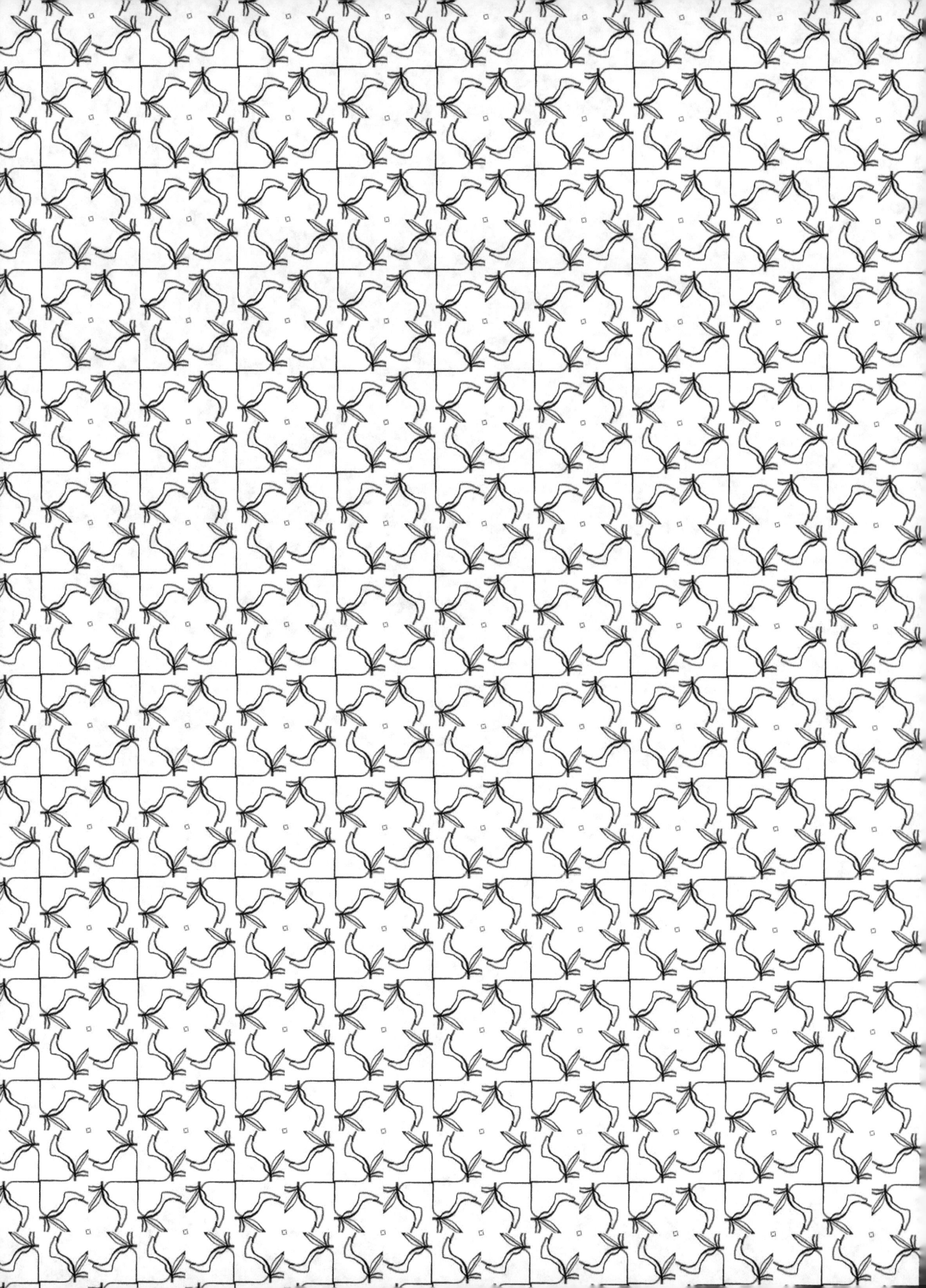

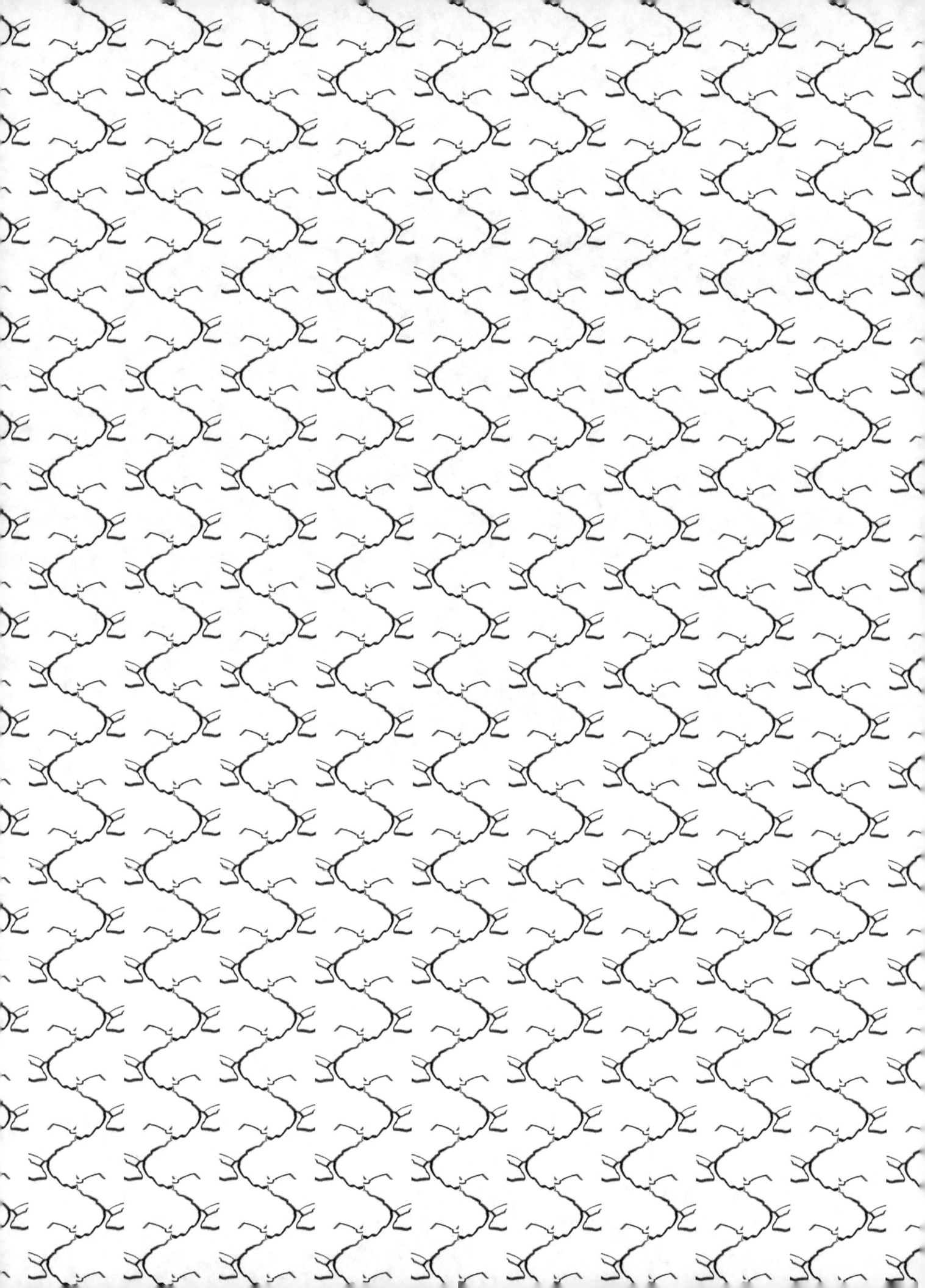

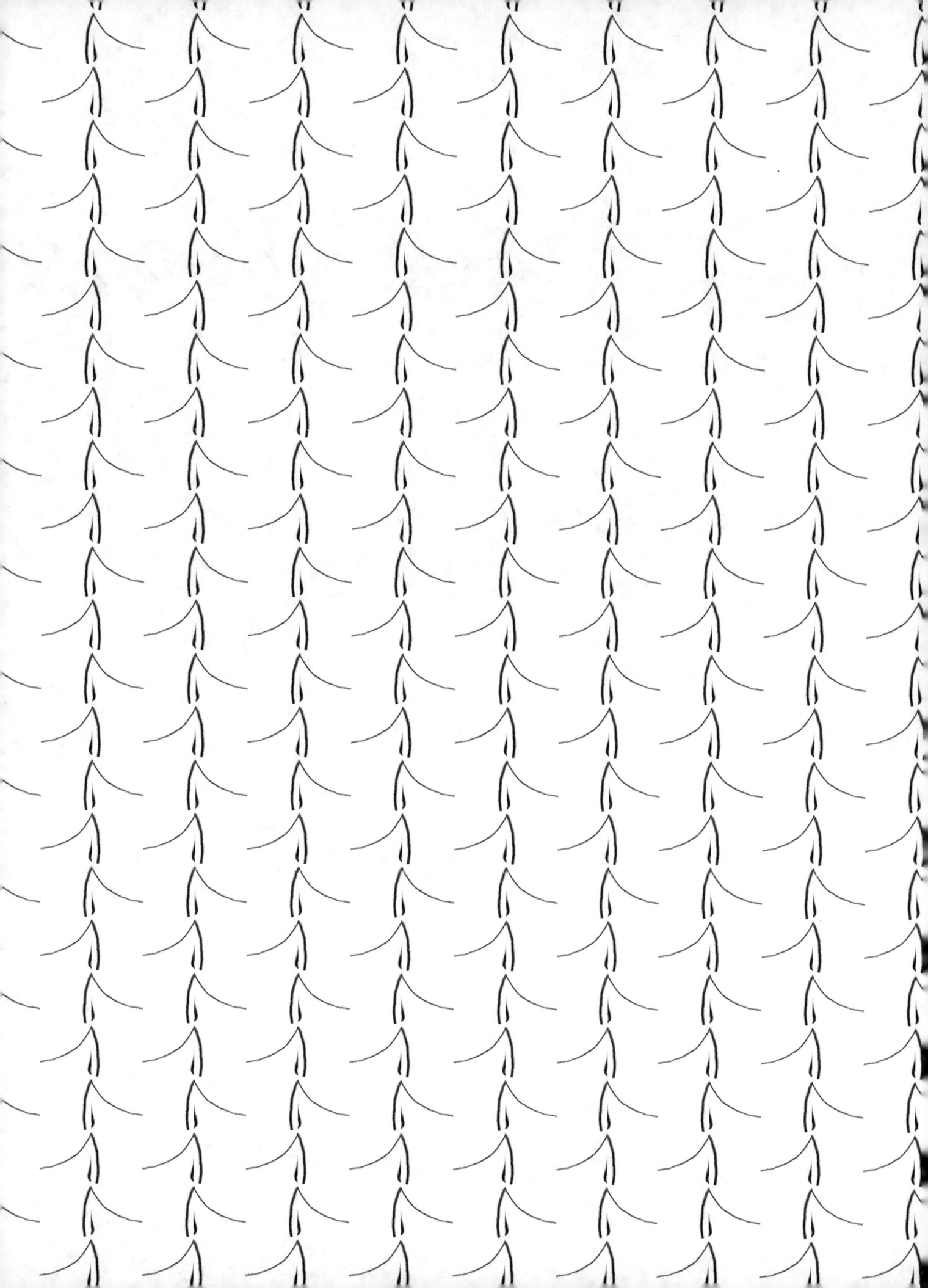

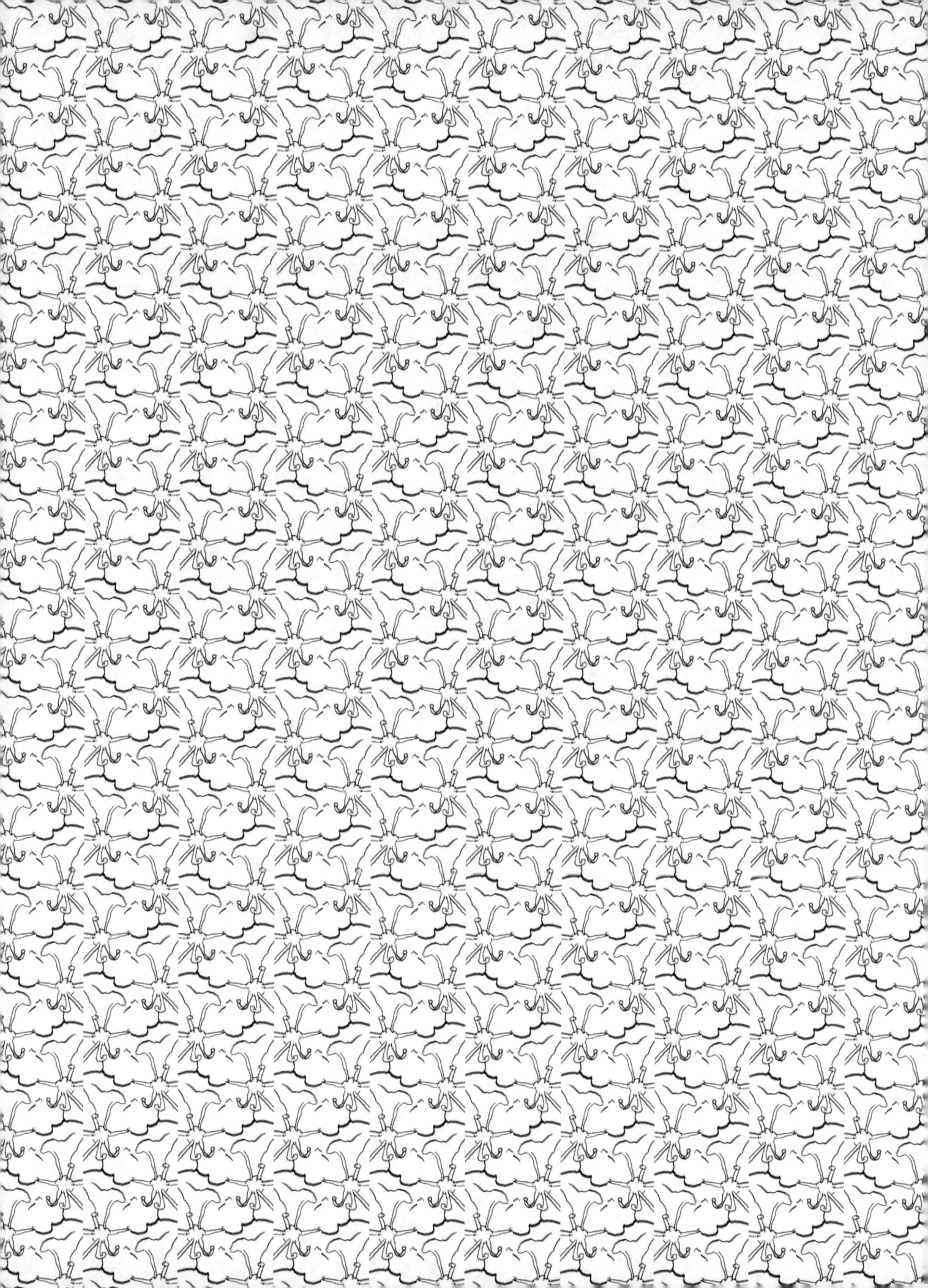

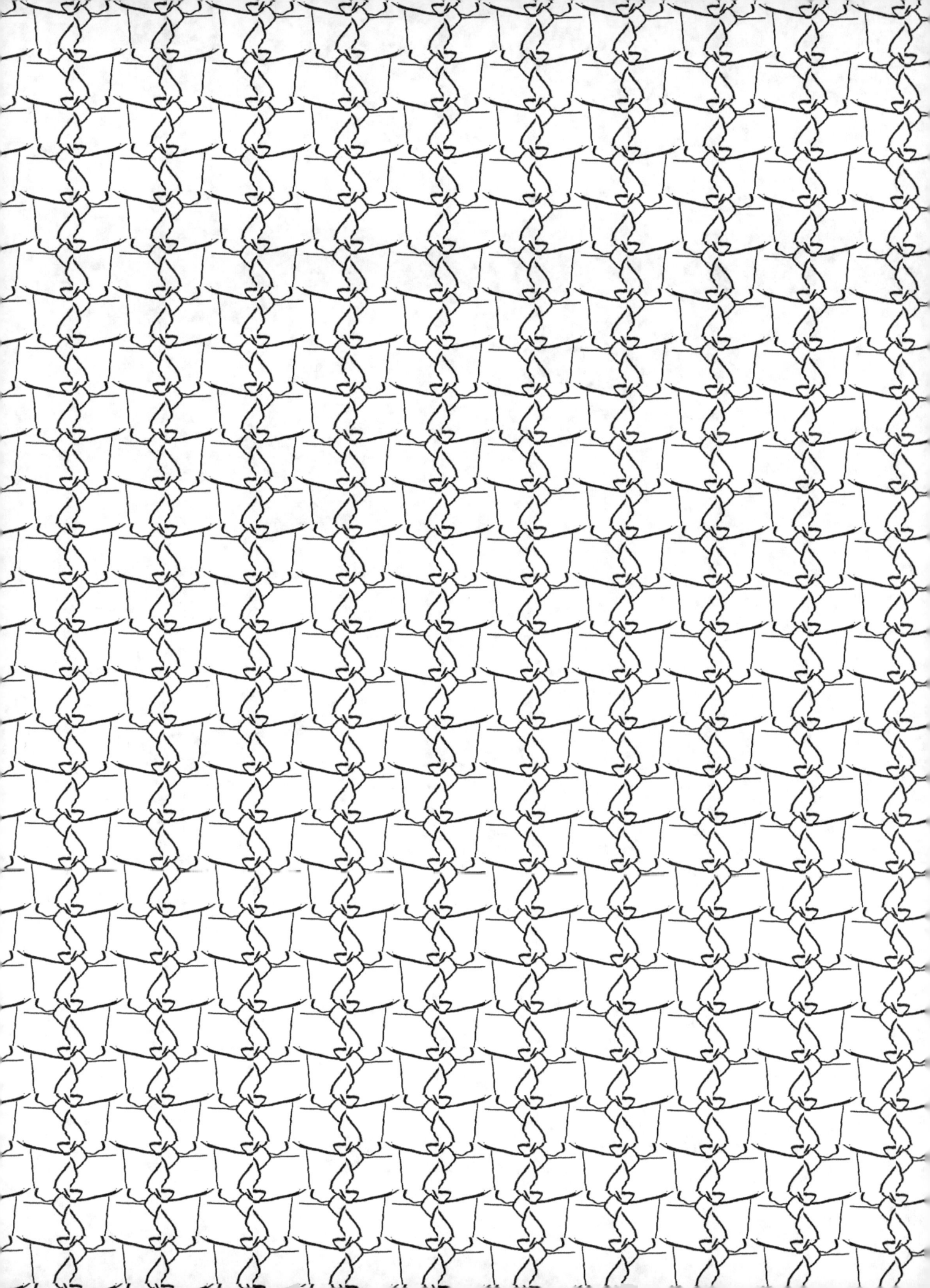

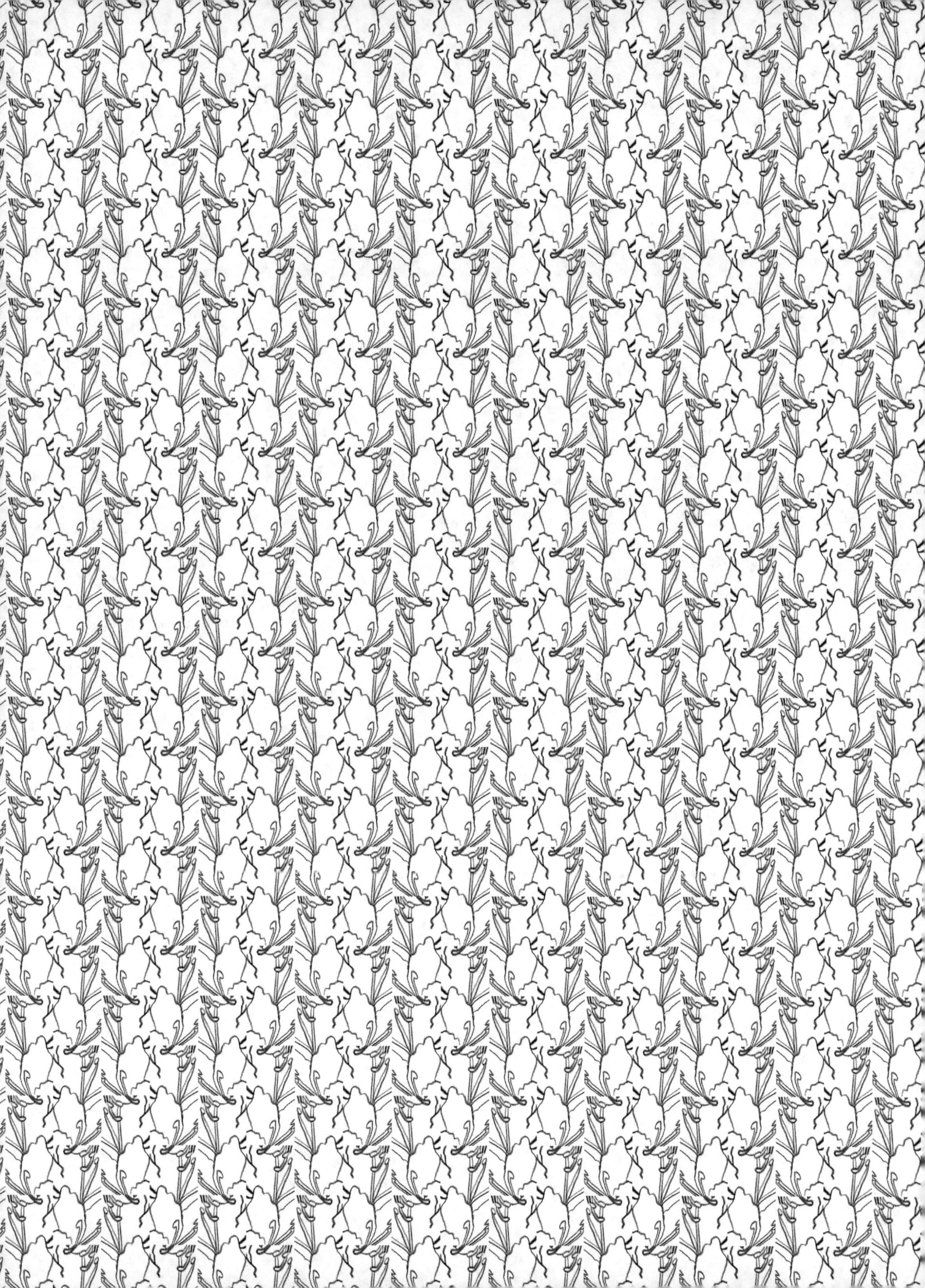

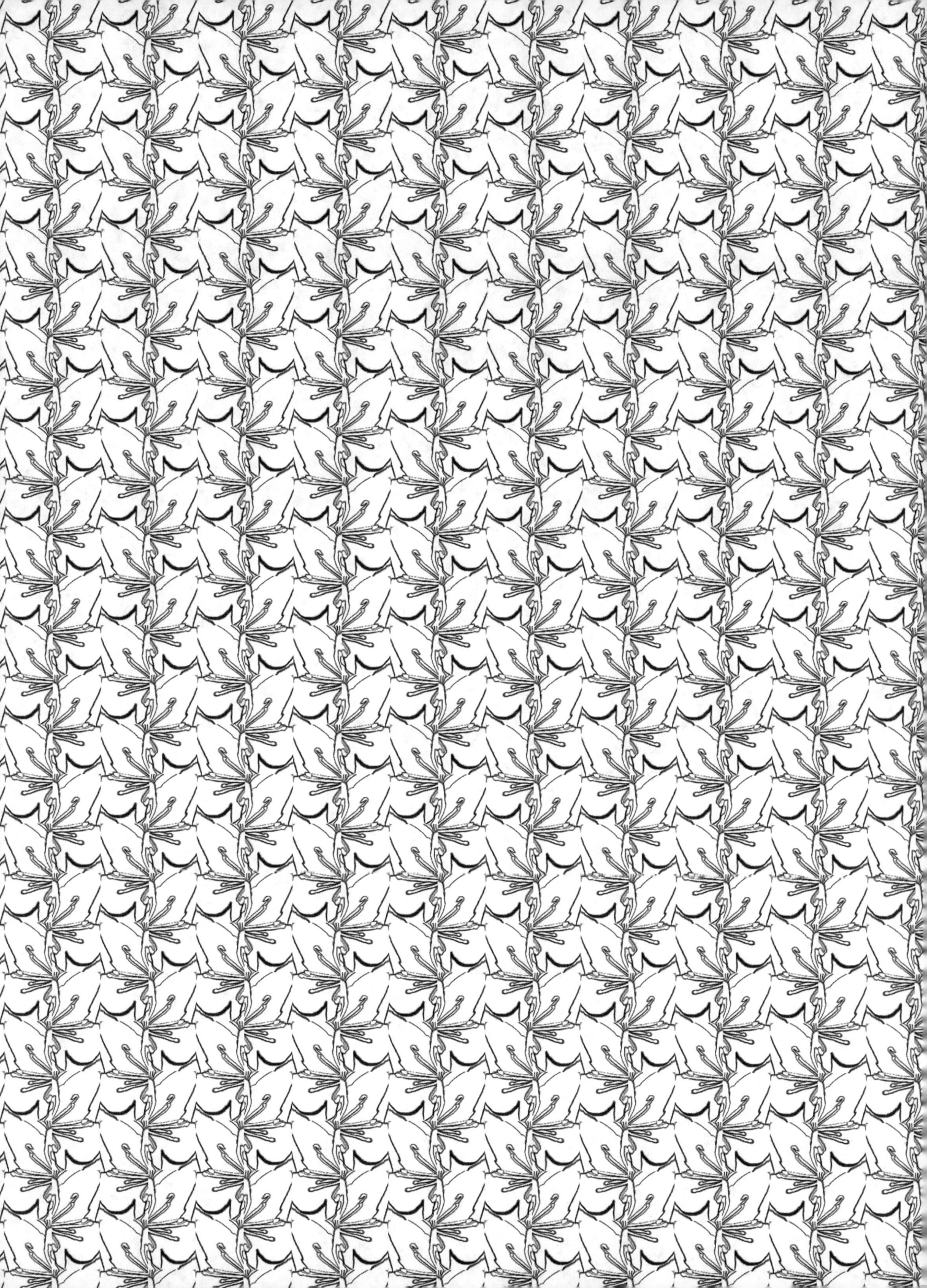

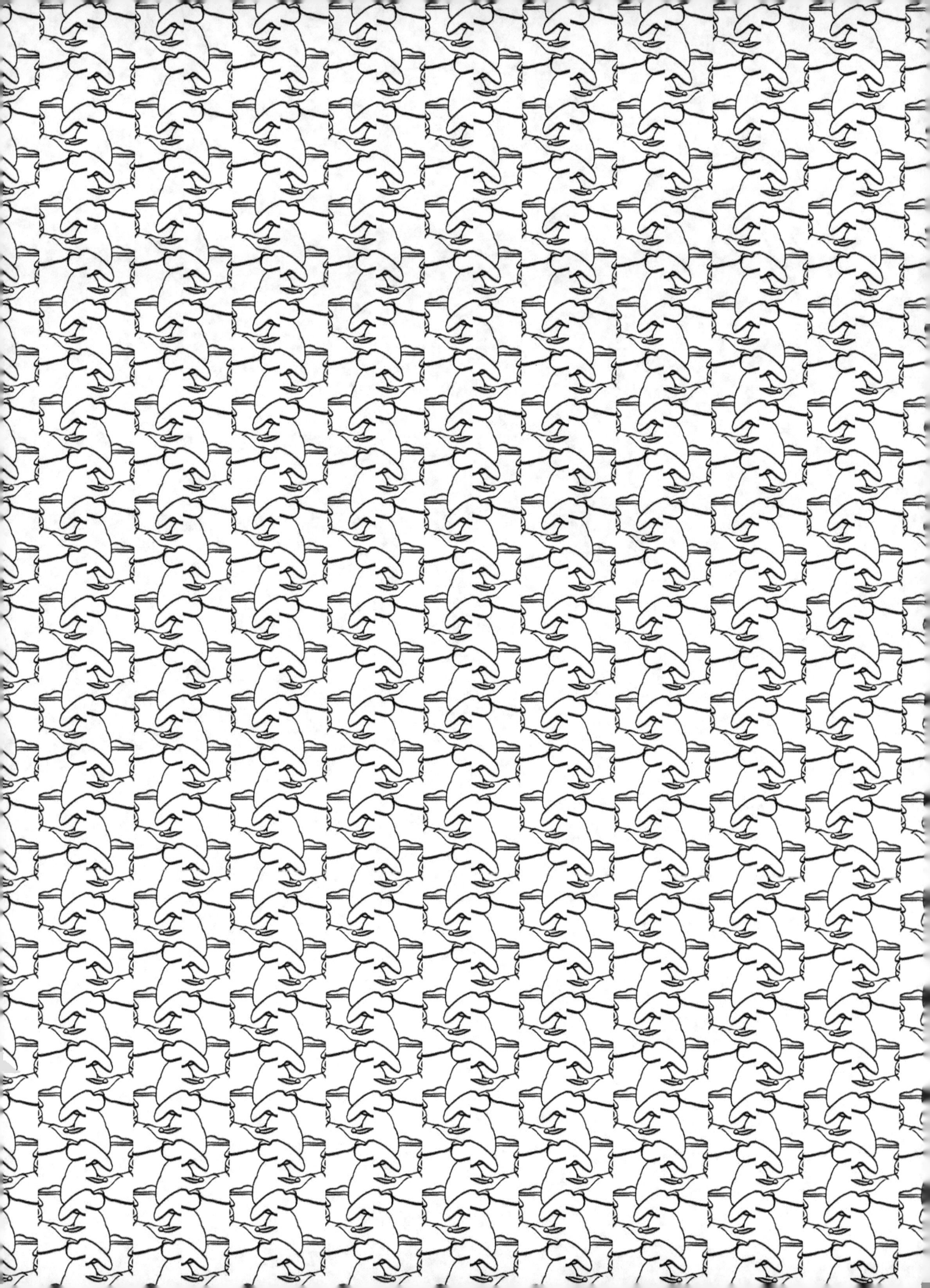

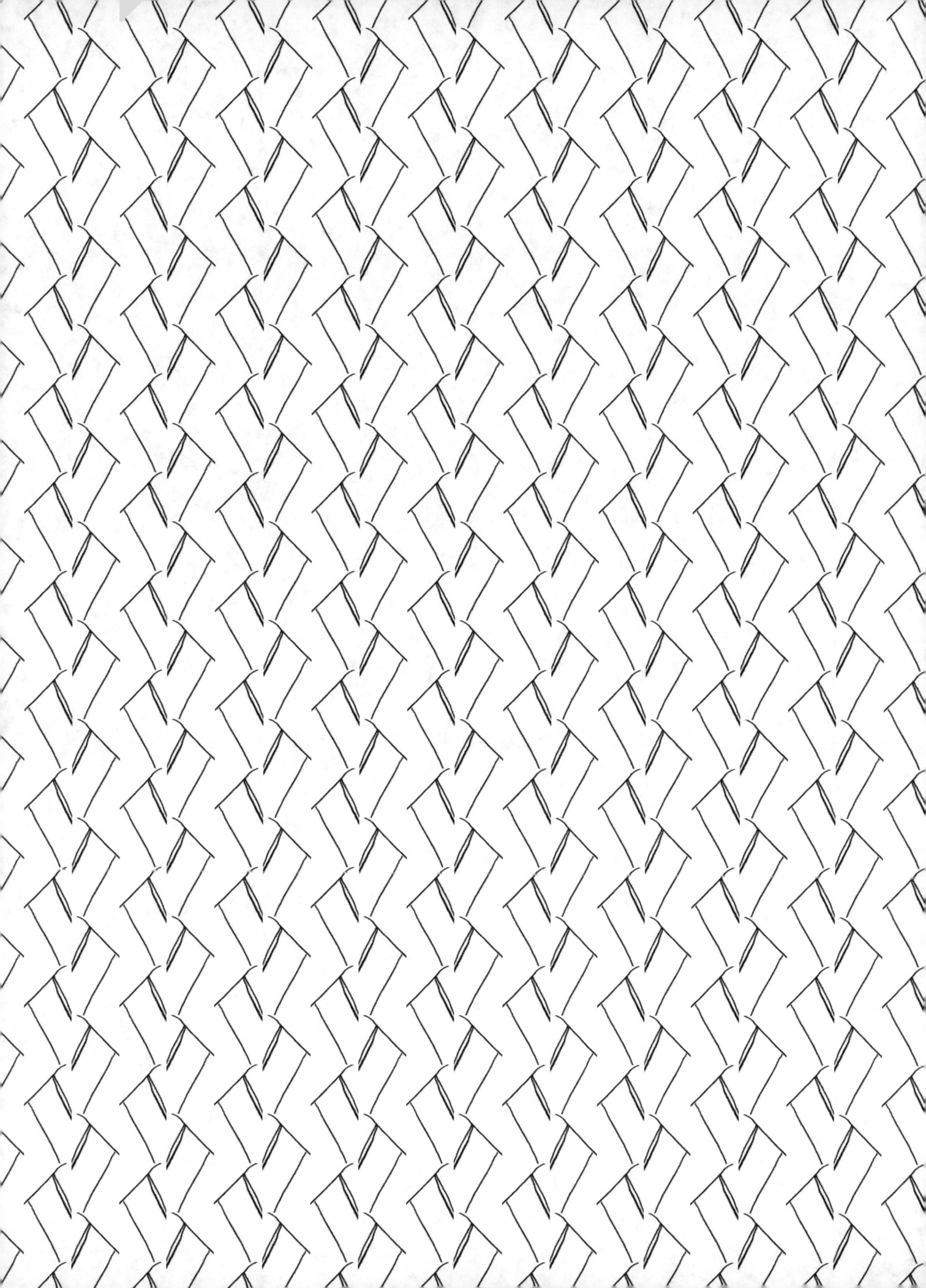

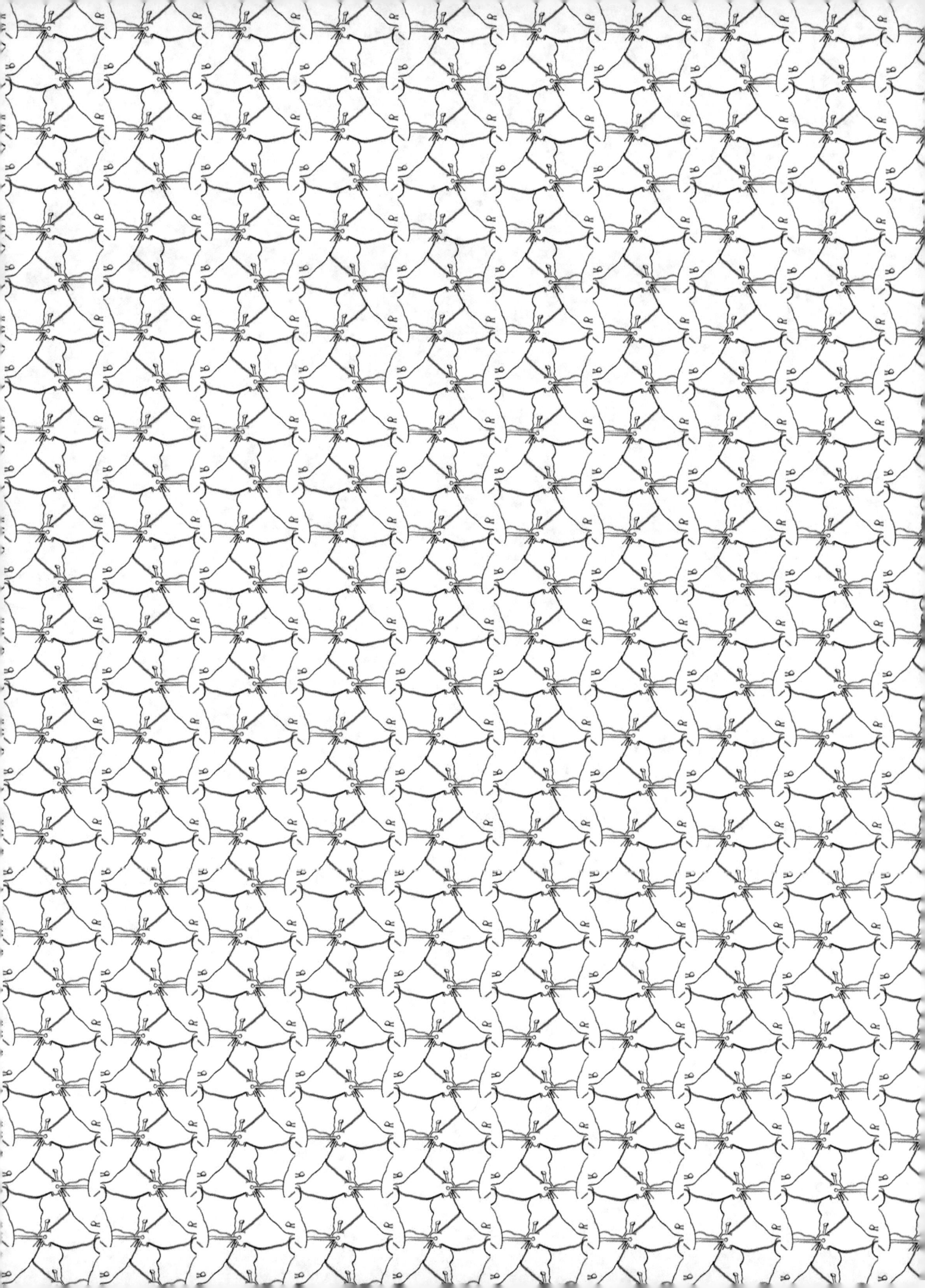

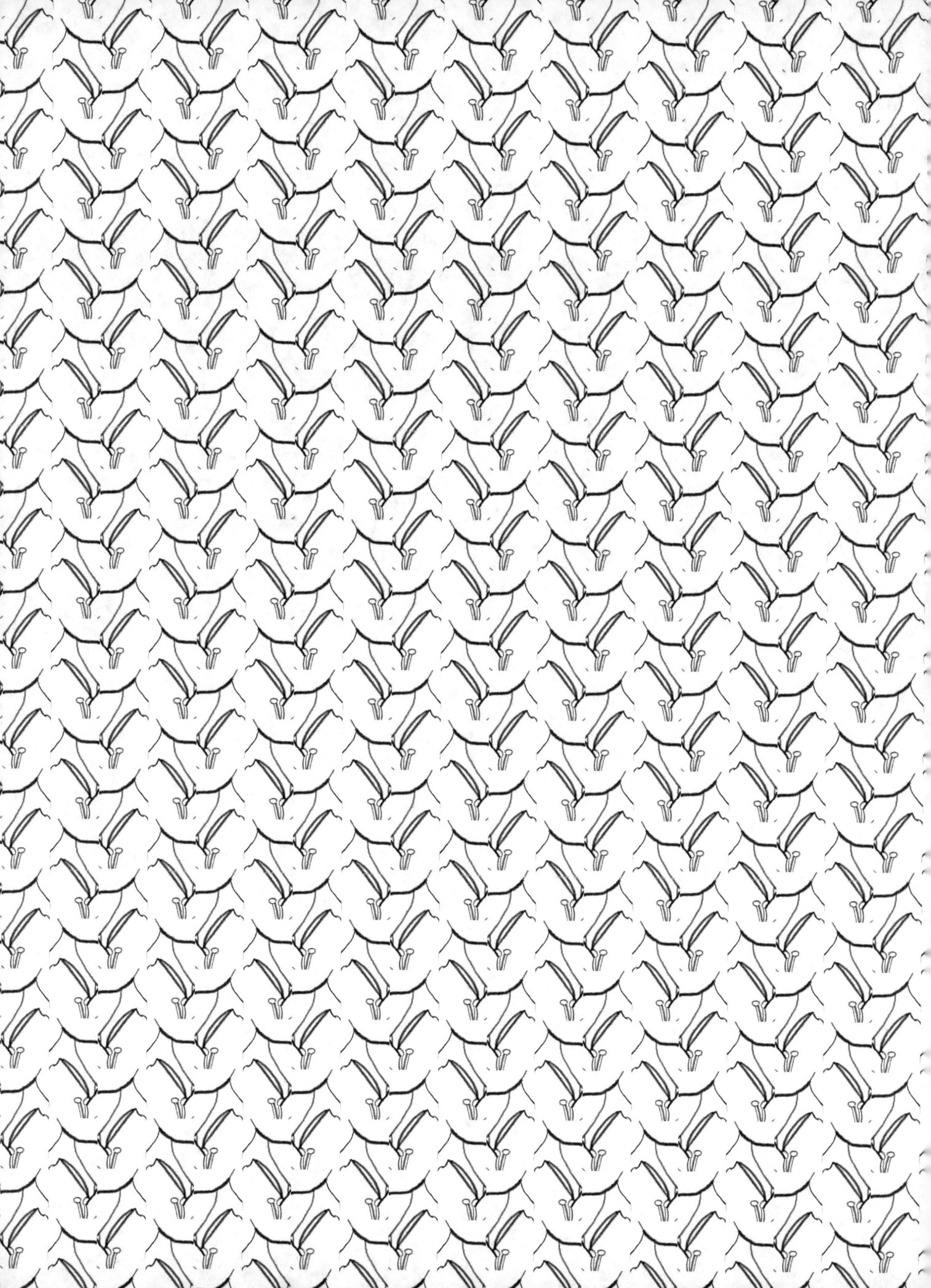

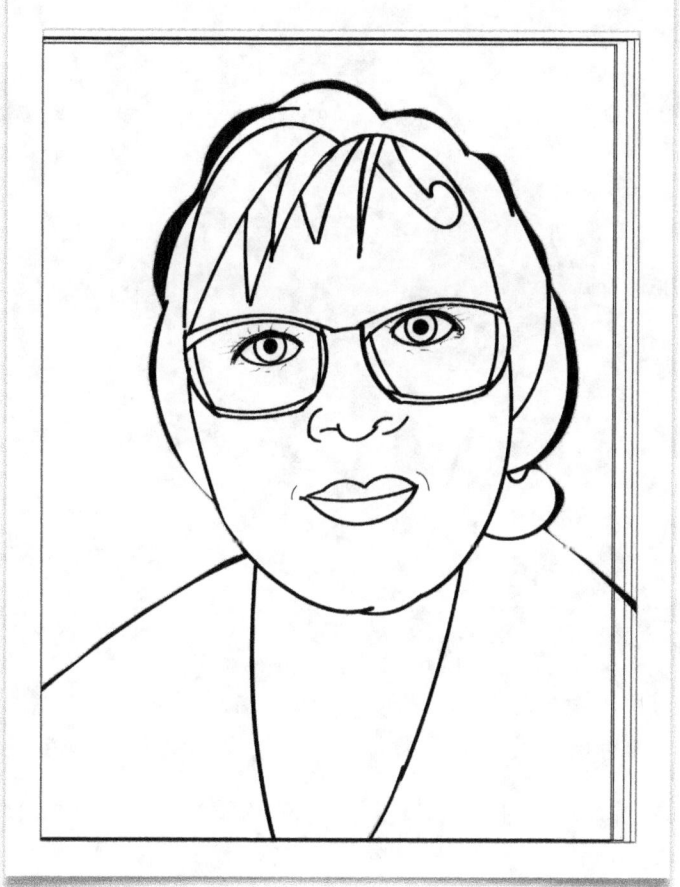

Dear Colorist,

I hope you have enjoyed this coloring book. It would be great if you would take a moment and review it on GoodReads.com or at the retailer where you bought it from.

Hope to hear from you.

Lily

www.LilyFrizz.com

@LilyFrizz (on Twitter)

www.LilyFrizz.com

www.ingramcontent.com/pod-product-compliance
Lightning Source LLC
Chambersburg PA
CBHW081158180526

45170CB00006B/2131